AMERICA'S BEST RV COOKBOOK

Joyce Ryan

BUTTERFLY
B O O K S

Published by Butterfly Books
4210 Misty Glade
San Antonio, Texas 78247
Telephone 210-494-0077

Email texaswavelady@hotmail.com

Manufactured in the United States of America

Library of Congress Cataloging-in-Publication Data

Ryan, Joyce.
  America's best RV cookbook : the complete guide to RV cooking / Joyce Ryan.
      p. cm.
Includes bibliographical references and index.
ISBN 0-939077-07-8 (pbk.)
  1. Cookery. 2. Mobile home living. I. Title

TX840.M6.R93 2003
641.5--dc21   2002033013

CONTENTS

Introduction

CHAPTER 1
Supplies and Equipment 6

CHAPTER 2
Appetizers 14

CHAPTER 3
Breads 22

CHAPTER 4
Main Dishes 48

CHAPTER 5
Side Dishes 119

CHAPTER 6
Desserts 155

CHAPTER 7
Substitutions and
Equivalents 186

CHAPTER 8
Common Problems 195

Resources 198
Bibliography 201
Index 202

DEDICATION
To Jim and Monet, of course

ALSO BY JOYCE RYAN
Happy Camper's Gourmet Cookbook
America's Best Cheesecakes
Drawing at Home
Calligraphy: Elegant and Easy
Traveling with Your Sketchbook
Seoul Travel Guide
Scenes of Southern Arizona
Seoul Sketches

ACKNOWLEDGMENTS
My appreciation and thanks go to Corinne Price-Keys for her intelligent editorial assistance. I give my very special thanks to Jim Klar for his helpful criticism and professional advise, and to Mother, the best cook in the world, for teaching me how to cook and instilling in me the desire to excel.

INTRODUCTION

We're on the road again! The thrill and excitement of a RV camping trip always fills me with anticipation. For me, camping trips are very special vacations, because the freedom that I feel is so exhilarating. Every journey rewards me with unique experiences and adventures just as invigorating as our first trip.

Much to my surprise, I discovered on our first trip that cooking in a RV was also an adventure. Preparing meals in a camper was more complicated than I had imagined. Although my camper kitchen was similar to my kitchen at home, I discovered firsthand an obvious difference. Restricted space made food preparation, cooking, and storage difficult. Because I believe that the quality of a trip is often influenced by the quality of the food, I've been determined since my first trip to prepare camper meals that are just as delicious as what I prepare at home.

With time and practice, I adapted favorite recipes to RV cooking that are simple, quick-to-prepare, and use as few ingredients as possible. My goal was delicious no-fuss food without sacrificing flavor for convenience. I wanted camping vacations to be a time to relax and to enjoy beautiful surroundings, not to stress-out in the kitchen.

During the past twenty years I've tested many recipes and gained considerable experience. The information I've accumulated and present here promises to make your next journey more enjoyable by providing you with 381 easy-to-prepare recipes that are especially adapted to RV cooking. For your convenience, I include tasty, full menu suggestions for main dishes. You will avoid typical camper kitchen problems by following my helpful hints for choosing basic supplies and equipment. My extensive food substitution list will prepare you for the inevitable problem of missing an important ingredient when you are in the boondocks or just too tired to shop.

The practical information and thoroughly tested recipes in this book will help you to successively combine your love of camping and good food.

HAPPY TRAILS TO YOU!

1
SUPPLIES AND EQUIPMENT

Choosing basic pantry supplies and essential kitchen equipment are important decisions, because RVs have limited storage space. These decisions are highly individual since they are based on taste preferences and personal cooking style. Analyzing your needs before going on a trip will reduce frustration and save time. I recommend that you make a detailed list of supplies and equipment based on the following guidelines.

SUPPLIES

Frequently used items have top priority. However, remember to include occasionally used items and favorite brands that might be difficult to obtain if you plan to travel to remote areas. Repackage items that are sold in large containers into smaller containers to increase the variety of on-hand supplies. Content labels are recommended for easy identification.

Place frequently used items in convenient locations. Seldom used items are best stored in clear plastic storage boxes in less accessible areas. Group like items in one area if possible. For example, all of my baking supplies are placed on one shelf.

Modular refrigerator-to-microwave containers are well-suited to RV food storage. Breakage is minimized, and they use space efficiently because they are stackable. These containers are invaluable for storing dry foods such as flour, sugar, rice, pasta, etc. They do double-duty when storing reheatable leftovers.

Restocking your supplies is a snap in urban areas. However, if you dislike hunting for ingredients in an unfamiliar grocery store, plan in advance by stocking additional supplies.

Base your quantities of supplies on how frequently you like to shop. Keep in mind the difficulty of restocking when camping in a remote area for an extended time.

Making a basic supply list will save you considerable time and frustration. The list provides a foolproof method of stocking your camper and prevents

you from forgetting essential items. The list also provides an effortless, convenient way to assess stock during a trip.

I recommend making photocopies of your basic supply list to take on trips. Tape the list inside a cabinet and check supplies as they become depleted. This method has enabled me to grab the list and head for the store on a moment's notice.

MASTER SUPPLY LIST

The following products are the ingredients I use in the recipes of this cookbook. Scan this extensive list, noting your requirements. Prepare a personalized basic supply list based on your preferences. Add timesavers, if desired (page 194).

Incidentally, my basic supply list features 50 items. For me, this is a very adequate variety of ingredients for weekend and one-week trips. For longer trips I include more items based on the length of the trip and particular menus that I want to prepare.

BAKING/STAPLES
Flour
Wheat flour
White/yellow cornmeal
Baking mix
Cornstarch
Sugar
Powdered sugar
Brown sugar
Yeast
Baking soda
Baking powder
Italian bread crumbs
Vegetable oil
Olive oil
Shortening
Nonstick cooking spray
Butter-flavored nonstick
  cooking spray
Evaporated milk
Sweetened condensed milk
Unsweetened cocoa powder
Unsweetened chocolate
Semisweet chocolate
Sweet baking chocolate
White chocolate baking bar
Cinnamon chips
Semisweet chocolate chips
Miniature semisweet
  chocolate chips
Butterscotch chips

Milk chocolate chips
Peanut butter chips
White baking chips
Toffee bits/English toffee
  bits
White chocolate chunks
Semisweet chocolate chunks
Vanilla extract
Almond extract
Imitation black walnut
  extract
Imitation coconut extract
Imitation maple extract
Orange extract
Imitation rum extract
Mint extract
Nuts
Canned pie filling
Food color
Spices and dried herbs

BAKERY
Bagels
Bread
English muffins
Hamburger/hot dog buns
Pita breads
Rolls
Tortillas
Crackers
Cookies

BEVERAGES
Coffee
Instant coffee
Instant espresso powder
Tea
Milk
Non-dairy creamer
Fruit juices
Soda
Wine
Beer
Liquor
Liqueur

CANNED/DRIED VEGETABLES AND FRUITS
Artichoke hearts
Beets
Cream-style corn
Whole kernel corn
Black beans
Great northern beans
Green beans
Navy beans
Pork and beans
Red kidney beans
Refried beans
Black-eyed peas
Hearts of palm

7

Mushrooms
Peas
Pumpkin
Tomatoes
Mexican-style tomatoes
Water chestnuts
Sliced apples
Blueberries
Candied fruit
Dried cranberries
Whole berry cranberry
  sauce
Coconut
Maraschino cherries
Dates
Mincemeat
Crushed pineapple in
  syrup
Raisins

CONDIMENTS/ SNACKS

Mayonnaise/salad dressing
Salad dressings
Spaghetti sauce
Barbecue sauce
Salsa
Picante sauce
Steak sauce
Worcestershire sauce
Soy sauce
Dry sherry
Liquid smoke
Ketchup
Chili sauce
Prepared mustard
Dijon mustard
Beef/chicken bouillon
Beef/chicken bouillon
  cubes
Beef/chicken broth
Chicken bouillon granules
Consommé
Tomato soup
Cream of chicken soup
Cream of mushroom soup
Cream of potato soup
Tomato paste
Tomato sauce
Lemon juice

Lime juice
Balsamic vinegar
Cider vinegar
White vinegar
Red/white wine vinegar
Rice vinegar
Capers
Pickles
Black olives
Pimiento-stuffed
  green olives
Marinated artichoke hearts
Jalapeños
Green chiles
Pimientos
Anchovy paste
Tahini
Peanut butter
Nutella
Jams/preserves
Honey
Popcorn
Potato chips/tortilla chips
Chocolate-flavored syrup
Maple syrup
Corn syrup
Molasses
Parmesan cheese
Process cheese spread loaf
  (such as Velveeta®)
Marshmallows
Marshmallow creme
Candy bars

DAIRY CASE

Milk
Cream
Half-and-half
Sour cream
Yogurt
Sliced process
  American cheese
Cheese
Cottage cheese
Cream cheese
Prepared horseradish
Eggs
Butter
Margarine
Refrigerated crescent rolls

Refrigerated buttermilk
  biscuits
Refrigerated sugar cookie
  dough

FROZEN FOODS

Fruit juices
Vegetables
Fruits
Non-dairy whipped
  topping
Ice cream
Frozen yogurt

MEAT/FISH

Beef
Ground beef
Chicken
Cornish hen
Duck
Ham
Pork
Bacon
Turkey bacon
Sausage
Turkey sausage
Smoked sausage links
Kielbasa
Pepperoni
Hot dogs
Turkey
Ground turkey
Fish
Shrimp
Luncheon meats
Tuna (canned)
Salmon (canned)
Crabmeat (canned)
Clams (canned)

MISCELLANEOUS SUPPLIES

Bath soap
Toiletries
Cleaning supplies
Sponges and pot scrubbers
Dishwashing liquid
Paper towels
Napkins
Facial tissue

Coffee filters
Toilet paper
Aluminum foil
Plastic wrap
Wax paper
Reclosable plastic bags
Garbage bags and ties
Paper plates
Paper cups
Plastic knifes, forks,
   and spoons
Toothpicks
Butane lighter
Matches
Laundry detergent
Holding tank supplies
Insect repellent
Sunscreen

PASTA/GRAINS/ CEREALS

Breakfast cereals
Oat bran cereal

Old-fashioned oats
Quick-cooking oats
Wheat germ
Fettucine
Spaghetti
Macaroni
Manicotti
Orzo
Egg noodles
Lasagne
Rotini
Rice
Wild rice

PRODUCE

Apples
Bananas
Cantaloupe
Cranberries
Lemons
Limes
Oranges
Peaches

Strawberries
Artichokes
Avocados
Broccoli
Green beans
Cauliflower
Carrots
Celery
Cucumber
Garlic
Green onions
Lettuce
Mushrooms
Onions
Potatoes
Green/red bell peppers
Radishes
Sweet potatoes
Tomatoes
Crookneck squash
Zucchini
Fresh herbs

EQUIPMENT

"Less is more," said Mies Van der Rohe. Remember his wise philosophy when selecting equipment for your RV. Take only the tools and utensils that are absolutely essential for your cooking needs; leave everything else at home.

Make certain that the baking pans and dishes you use in your oven and microwave and the storage containers you use in your refrigerator actually fit them. RV ovens, microwaves, and refrigerators are considerably smaller than the ones in your kitchen.

Unless your equipment and supplies are securely stored, they will slip and slide when your vehicle is underway. Lining shelves with non-skid matting will reduce movement. For additional stability, fill empty spaces between items with rolled dish towels, paper towel rolls, or toilet paper rolls.

MASTER EQUIPMENT LIST

Scan this extensive equipment list then make your own list, adding or eliminating items based on what is critical to your cooking style. When you are satisfied with your list, make photocopies. Use the list to check-off items each time you load your RV. Minimize loading and unloading by stocking your RV with as many permanent items as possible.

Balance your load of equipment and supplies and avoid overpacking your RV. Check your vehicle's recommended weight capacity.

Obviously, weekend jaunts require less equipment than a six-month trek to Alaska. My basic equipment list includes 36 items. I use this list for weekend and one-week trips. When we take longer vacations, I expand the number of items.

COOKING

3 nonstick skillets (small, medium, and large)
Lid for large skillet
3 saucepans and lids (small, medium, and large)
1 stockpot and lid
Griddle
Grill pan
Coffeepot
Espresso coffeepot

GRILLING

Portable grill
Charcoal
Charcoal lighter fluid
Tongs
Heat-resistant mitt
Skewers
Grill basket
Grill fork

MECHANICAL AIDS

Drip coffeemaker
Toaster
Food processor
Hand-held electric mixer and beaters
Blender
Slow cooker
Microwave oven
Electric can opener
Electric skillet
Coffee grinder
Waffle iron
Indoor-outdoor grill
Electric burner

MIXING/MEASURING

3 mixing bowls (small, medium, and large), preferably microwavable
1 medium metal mixing bowl (I use this bowl for rising bread and pizza dough in a warm oven.)
Set of measuring spoons
Set of measuring cups
1-cup liquid measuring cup
2-cup liquid measuring cup
Sifter

EATING UTENSILS

Knifes, forks, and spoons
Nonbreakable dinnerware (plates, bowls, mugs, serving bowls, and platter)
Nonbreakable drinking glasses
Wine glasses
2 to 3 small and medium bowls for sauces and condiments, preferably microwavable

BAKING

13x9x1/2-inch shallow baking pan (turn pan upside down to use as a cookie sheet)
13x9x2-inch baking pan
11x7x2-inch baking dish (Pyrex® is preferred) NOTE: Use a baking pan to broil. Baking dishes should not be used in a broiler.
11x7x2-inch baking pan
9-inch square baking pan
8-inch square baking pan
8-inch square baking dish (Pyrex® is preferred)
8 1/2 x 4 1/2 x 2 1/2-inch loaf dish (Pyrex® is preferred)
8 1/2 x 4 1/2 x 2 1/2-inch loaf pan
9-inch round cake pan
8-inch round cake pan
9-inch springform pan
8-inch springform pan, optional (I use this pan for a favorite cake recipe)
12-inch pizza pan
Muffin pan

9-inch pie plate (Pyrex® is preferred)
2 to 3 pot holders
Wire rack

FOOD STORAGE
Cooler(s)
Small, medium, and large refrigerator-to-
microwave storage containers and lids
Modular pint and quart freezer containers
and lids (for freezer storage and for dry
food storage)
Canisters for flour, sugar, etc.
Fruit juice container for refrigerator
1 gallon plastic container for water
Water container for refrigerator
Salad dressing cruet
Pie/cakekeeper

UTENSILS
Spatula
2 to 3 wooden spoons
Slotted spoon
Ladle
Small and large knifes
Large serrated knife
Rolling pin (nonbreakable drinking
glass with straight sides can be
substituted)
Can opener
Vegetable peeler
Grater/zester
Potato masher
Corkscrew
Wooden mallet
Instant-read thermometer
Oven thermometer
Refrigerator thermometer
Small and large strainers
Colander
Cutting board
Swiss knife

MISCELLANEOUS
Clear plastic storage boxes and
lids, assorted sizes
Tote bags
Ice cube trays
Cold packs
Dish pan
Dish cloth and dish towels

Linens
Sewing kit and scissors
First aid kit
Fire extinguisher
Extension cords
Thermos
Mini-vacuum cleaner
Broom
Mop
Iron
Fly swatter
Flashlight and batteries
Batteries
Stationary and stamps
Address book
Cell phone/charger
Travel information/maps
Money/traveler's checks
Medicines
Tool kit

PET SUPPLIES
Food and treats
Bowls for water and food
Grooming supplies
Shampoo
Leash
Medicines
Flea powder
Toys
Vaccination records

RECREATION
Arts and crafts supplies
Books/magazines
Camera and film
CDs and tapes
Fishing equipment
Games/playing cards
Sports equipment

EXTRA TOUCHES
Candles and candle holders
Cloth napkins
Napkin rings
Flower vase
Place mats
Table cloth
Trays

EMERGENCY FOOD AND EQUIPMENT

Be advised that some camping locations will not have electricity. If you don't have a generator, you will need to plan for those occasions by including additional equipment. For example, if you rely on an electric can opener and an electric coffeemaker, include a manual can opener and an espresso coffeepot.

On the other hand, I've also had the misfortune of running out of propane at inopportune times, usually in the midst of preparing a meal. At these times, an electric skillet or an extra electric burner has saved the day.

Although at most camping locations you have access to a wide variety of fresh foods, be prepared for unusual circumstances. Out-of-the-way stores are not restocked as efficiently as urban stores; they frequently run out of milk, bread, and produce. Stock non-dairy creamer, extra crackers, and dried or canned fruit in your RV pantry.

ADVANCED FOOD PREPARATION

When deciding what to eat on your vacation, consider cooking some meals at home before your trip. Planning ahead simplifies camp cooking. Foods such as stews, soups, sauces, and meatballs can be prepared at home and frozen. Beef and chicken can be precooked and cut into bite-size pieces to aid in the preparation of stews and casseroles at camp.

The amount of food that you precook depends, of course, on the capacity of your freezer and refrigerator. Even if available space is limited, try to include at least one pre-cooked meal. I've found that the first-night dinner practically ready to eat when you pull into camp is especially appreciated after a long day's drive.

Another time- and energy-saving tip is to premix dry ingredients for meat rubs, brownies, and corn bread and place them in reclosable bags for easy use. When at camp, you can stir in the wet ingredients. I also premix breading for fish and chicken and store these mixtures in reclosable bags in the refrigerator.

RV OVENS AND REFRIGERATORS

Your RV's oven and refrigerator may not be as reliable as those in your home.

Regulating your oven's temperature is often a challenge. Place an oven thermometer in the oven to determine if its actual temperature corresponds to the temperature you set with the dial. The temperature of some ovens fluctuates during baking, increasing or decreasing during the baking process. Periodically check the thermometer to monitor the temperature.

If you notice that cookies, pizza, and other baked goods often burn on the bottom before done, try baking with two sheets/pans stacked one on top of the other to shield the cookies from excess heat. If preferred, purchase insulated (air-cushioned) baking sheets, because they also shield from excess heat.

If you enjoy baking, you'll find adapting to your oven's quirks is rewarding. Nothing beats the homemade flavors and aromas of freshly baked breads and desserts.

Many RV refrigerators can only reduce the temperature to 40–60° below the outside temperature. To ensure food safety, keep a refrigerator thermometer in the refrigerator and check it occasionally. This precaution will help you to know whether the food is chilled sufficiently to avoid spoilage.

As a safety measure, I keep several cold packs in the freezer at all times. During a very hot day, I transfer them to the refrigerator portion to help lower the temperature. At night, I return them to the freezer so that they will be ready for the next day. Cold packs are also useful in the initial start-up of your refrigerator before a trip. They enable the refrigerator to reach a safe temperature more rapidly.

Since your RV refrigerator isn't as efficient as the refrigerator in your home, preserve a safe interior temperature by opening the door as seldom as possible. Placing beverages in a cooler reduces the need to open the door and offers the added benefit of increased cold storage capacity.

SAFETY TIPS

Resist the temptation to cook while your RV is under way. Regardless of whether you are using a slow cooker or an enclosed oven, an unexpected stop or sharp turn could send the pot and its contents flying or cause the oven door to open. Also, gas flames are dangerous. If you become involved in an accident in which propane or gasoline is leaking, the consequences could prove disastrous.

2
APPETIZERS

GREEN CHILE CHEESE BALL   6 to 8 servings

8 ounces shredded extra sharp Cheddar cheese (2 cups)
1 package (8 ounces) cream cheese, softened
1/4 cup canned chopped green chiles, drained
2 teaspoons ground cumin
3/4 teaspoon garlic powder, scant
Garnish: Chili powder and dried parsley flakes

1. Mix all ingredients in medium bowl until blended.
2. Shape cheese mixture into ball. Roll in mixture of chili powder and parsley. Cover and refrigerate until firm. Serve with crackers.

PESTO CHEESE BALL   4 servings

1 package (8 ounces) cream cheese, softened
1/2 cup pesto

1. Mix cream cheese and pesto in medium bowl until blended.
2. Shape cheese mixture into ball. Cover and refrigerate until firm. Serve with crackers.

GOUDA CHEESE BALL   6 servings

7 ounces shredded Gouda cheese (1 3/4 cups)
1 package (8 ounces) cream cheese, softened
1 tablespoon caraway seed
1/4 teaspoon coarse black pepper

1. Place all ingredients in food processor. Cover and blend on high speed, stopping processor occasionally to scrape sides, until smooth.
2. Shape cheese mixture into ball. Cover and refrigerate until firm. Serve with crackers.

BLUE CHEESE-GARLIC CHEESE BALL   4 servings

1 package (8 ounces) cream cheese, cut into cubes
1/2 cup crumbled blue cheese (2 ounces)
3/4 teaspoon minced garlic

1. Place cream cheese, blue cheese, and garlic in microwavable bowl. Heat in microwave on High (100%) until softened, stopping and stirring, until smooth.
2. Cover and refrigerate until firm. Shape cheese mixture into ball. Serve with crackers or sliced French bread.

MONTEREY JACK CHEESE BALL   6 to 8 servings

8 ounces shredded Monterey Jack cheese (2 cups)
1 package (8 ounces) cream cheese, softened
1/2 teaspoon coarse black pepper
1/4 teaspoon garlic powder
1/4 teaspoon salt

1. Mix all ingredients in medium bowl until blended.
2. Shape cheese mixture into ball. Cover and refrigerate until firm. Serve with crackers.

MONTEREY JACK-HERB CHEESE BALL: Reduce black pepper to 1/4 teaspoon. Omit salt. Add 1 teaspoon dried dill weed, 1 teaspoon dried chives, 1/2 teaspoon dried basil leaves, and 1/2 teaspoon dried parsley flakes.

PEPPER-JACK CHEESE BALL: Substitute 8 ounces shredded Monterey Jack cheese with jalapeños for Monterey Jack cheese.

SALSA AND BLACK BEAN DIP   6 servings

1 can (15 to 16 ounces) black beans, drained
1 1/2 cups salsa

Mix black beans and salsa. Serve with tortilla chips.

BLACK BEAN DIP   4 servings

1 can (15 to 16 ounces) black beans, rinsed and drained
6 tablespoons picante sauce
1 large clove garlic, minced
1/2 teaspoon chili powder
1/2 teaspoon ground cumin
1/4 teaspoon dried oregano leaves
1/4 teaspoon salt
1/8 teaspoon coarse black pepper

Place all ingredients in food processor. Cover and blend on high speed, stopping processor occasionally to scrape sides, until smooth. Serve with tortilla chips.

NEW YEAR'S DAY   8 servings
BLACK-EYED PEA DIP

1 can (15 ounces) black-eyed peas, rinsed and drained
1 package (8 ounces) cream cheese, softened
1/4 cup chopped green onions
1/4 cup chopped onion
1 large clove garlic, minced
1 1/2 teaspoons chili powder
3/4 teaspoon salt
1/2 teaspoon garlic powder
1/2 teaspoon coarse black pepper
1/4 teaspoon garlic salt
Garnish: Shredded Cheddar cheese

Place all ingredients in food processor. Cover and blend on high speed, stopping processor occasionally to scrape sides, until smooth. Spoon mixture into glass or plastic bowl. Garnish with Cheddar cheese. Serve with tortilla chips.

SALSA   about 1 1/2 cups

1 can (14 1/2 ounces) whole tomatoes, drained
1/3 cup canned tomato sauce
1/4 cup chopped onion

2 tablespoons canned chopped green chiles
2 teaspoons white vinegar
1 teaspoon chili powder
1/2 teaspoon minced garlic

Coarsely chop tomatoes and drain. Mix all ingredients in small glass or plastic bowl. Serve with tortilla chips.

VEGGIE SALSA   4 to 6 servings

1 can (14 1/2 ounces) whole tomatoes, drained
1/2 cup chopped zucchini
1/2 cup chopped onion
1/2 cup chopped celery
1/3 cup tomato sauce
1 tablespoon canned chopped green chile
2 teaspoons white vinegar
1 teaspoon chili powder
1 large clove garlic, minced
1/4 teaspoon salt
1/4 teaspoon coarse black pepper

Coarsely chop tomatoes and drain. Mix tomatoes and remaining ingredients in glass or plastic bowl. Serve with tortilla chips.

TEXAS CAVIAR   4 to 6 servings

1 can (15 to 16 ounces) black-eyed peas, rinsed and drained
1/2 cup chopped green onions
1/4 cup chopped green bell pepper
1/4 cup strained picante sauce
1 jar (2 ounces) chopped pimientos, drained (1/4 cup)
2 tablespoons red wine vinegar
1 tablespoon vegetable oil
1 1/2 teaspoons dry Italian dressing mix
1 teaspoon dried parsley flakes
1 large clove garlic, minced
1/4 teaspoon coarse black pepper

Mix all ingredients in medium glass or plastic bowl. Cover and refrigerate at least 8 hours to blend flavors. Serve with tortilla chips.

HUMMUS 　　　4 to 6 servings

1 can (15 ounces) garbanzo beans, rinsed and drained
3 tablespoons tahini (sesame paste)
3 tablespoons olive oil
2 tablespoons lemon juice
1 teaspoon minced garlic
1 teaspoon ground cumin
1/4 teaspoon salt
1/8 teaspoon coarse black pepper
Garnish: Fresh parsley sprigs

Place all ingredients in food processor. Cover and blend on high speed, stopping processor occasionally to scrape sides, until smooth. Place in glass or plastic bowl. Garnish with parsley sprigs. Serve with tortilla chips, raw vegetables, or pita bread (cut into triangles).

SOUTHWESTERN-STYLE 　　4 servings
BEAN DIP

1 can (15.8 ounces) great northern beans, rinsed and drained
1 1/2 teaspoons olive oil
1 1/2 teaspoons lemon juice
1 teaspoon minced garlic
1/4 teaspoon chili powder
1/4 teaspoon ground cumin
1/4 teaspoon salt
1/4 teaspoon coarse ground pepper
Garnish: Fresh parsley sprigs

Place all ingredients in food processor. Cover and blend on high speed, stopping processor occasionally to scrape sides, until smooth. Place in glass or plastic bowl. Garnish with parsley sprigs. Serve as a dip for tortilla chips or as a spread for French bread.

TOMATO-GARLIC SPREAD   4 servings

1 can (14 1/2 ounces) whole tomatoes, drained
1 tablespoon vegetable oil
1 tablespoon tomato paste
1 teaspoon minced garlic
1/2 teaspoon dried basil leaves
1/4 teaspoon dried oregano leaves
1/4 teaspoon salt
1/8 teaspoon coarse black pepper

1. Chop tomatoes and drain. Place tomatoes in single layer between double layer of paper towels. Press to remove juice.
2. Place tomatoes and remaining ingredients in food processor. Cover and blend on high speed, stopping processor occasionally to scrape sides, until smooth. Place in glass or plastic bowl. Serve immediately or cover and refrigerate until time to serve. Serve with sliced French bread.

ITALIAN PARSLEY SAUCE   4 to 6 servings

1/2 cup chopped green onions
1/2 cup chopped fresh parsley leaves
1/3 cup olive oil
2 tablespoons white wine vinegar, scant
1 1/2 teaspoons anchovy paste
1 teaspoon minced garlic
1/8 teaspoon salt
1/8 teaspoon coarse black pepper
2 tablespoons capers, drained

1. Place all ingredients except capers in food processor. Cover and blend on high speed, stopping processor occasionally to scrape sides, until smooth.
2. Transfer mixture to glass or plastic bowl. Stir in capers. Pour sauce onto individual serving plates. Dip cubes of French bread into sauce. Refrigerate any remaining sauce.

PICO DE GALLO   3 cups

2 to 3 medium peeled tomatoes, seeded and chopped (2 1/2 cups)
1/2 cup chopped green onions
1/2 cup chopped onion
3 tablespoons lime juice
2 tablespoons finely chopped fresh cilantro or parsley
1 tablespoon vegetable oil
1 to 3 tablespoons canned chopped green chiles
3/4 teaspoon salt

Mix all ingredients in medium glass or plastic bowl. Cover and refrigerate 3 hours or up to 24 hours. Drain before serving if thicker sauce is desired. Serve with tortilla chips.

COTTAGE CHEESE-DILL DIP   4 to 6 servings

1 carton (12 ounces) low-fat cottage cheese
2 tablespoons chopped green onion
1 tablespoon dried dill weed
2 teaspoons Worcestershire sauce
1 teaspoon dried parsley flakes
1/2 teaspoon garlic salt
1/8 teaspoon coarse black pepper

Place all ingredients in food processor. Cover and blend on high speed, stopping processor occasionally to scrape sides, until smooth. Serve with raw vegetables.

PICANTE DEVILED EGGS   4 servings

4 hard-cooked eggs, peeled
2 tablespoons strained picante sauce
1 tablespoon salad dressing or mayonnaise
1/8 teaspoon salt
1/8 teaspoon coarse black pepper
Garnish: Chopped pimientos

1. Cut eggs lengthwise in half. Slip out yolk and mash with fork.
2. Stir in picante sauce, salad dressing, salt, and pepper. Fill whites with egg yolk mixture, heaping it lightly. Cover and refrigerate up to 24 hours.

ITALIAN NACHOS   4 servings

Tortilla chips
1/2 cup chopped green bell pepper
1/2 cup halved black olives
8 to 10 cherry tomatoes, cut into fourths
1 1/2 ounces sliced pepperoni (about 24 slices)
5 ounces shredded mozzarella cheese (1 1/4 cups)
3 tablespoons grated Parmesan cheese

1. Heat oven to 400°. Line a 12-inch pizza pan with aluminum foil.
2. Place tortilla chips in single layer in pan. Sprinkle with remaining ingredients in order listed.
3. Bake 7 to 10 minutes or until cheese is melted. Serve on small plates.

CHESAPEAKE BAY   3 to 4 appetizer servings
SHRIMP COCKTAIL

1 can (12 ounces) beer (1 1/2 cups)
1/2 to 1 teaspoon Chesapeake Bay style seafood seasoning
2/3 pound uncooked medium shrimp, peeled and deveined
Chesapeake Bay Cocktail Sauce:
1/2 cup ketchup
1 teaspoon Chesapeake Bay style seafood seasoning

1. Heat beer and seafood seasoning to boiling in large saucepan. Add shrimp. Boil uncovered 3 to 5 minutes or until shrimp are pink and firm; drain.
2. While shrimp are boiling, mix ketchup and seafood seasoning. Serve shrimp with sauce.

FRICO

Freshly shredded Parmesan cheese (do not substitute canned grated
   Parmesan cheese)

Heat oven to 350°. Line a baking sheet with aluminum foil. Place small piles (1 tablespoon each) of cheese on the sheet, one to two inches apart. Press slightly to level. Bake 8 to 10 minutes or until crisp. Remove from oven. Cool 1 minute on sheet. Remove from sheet.

3
BREADS

PEANUT BUTTER SCONES   6 scones

1/3 cup creamy peanut butter
1/3 cup milk
3 tablespoons sugar
1 1/3 cups plus 2 tablespoons baking mix

1. Heat oven to 450°. Spray an 8-inch round cake pan with nonstick cooking spray.
2. Mix peanut butter, milk, and sugar until smooth. Stir in baking mix until soft dough forms. Divide dough into 6 pieces and drop onto a lightly floured surface. With floured hands, shape each piece into a ball. Place in pan.
3. Bake 10 to 15 minutes or until light brown. Cool in pan on wire rack. Serve with jam or preserves.

WHEAT GERM SCONES   6 scones

1 cup baking mix
1/3 cup wheat germ
1/4 cup packed light brown sugar
1/3 cup plus 1 tablespoon yogurt
Additional baking mix or yogurt, if needed

1. Heat oven to 400°. Spray an 8-inch round cake pan with nonstick cooking spray.
2. Mix all ingredients until soft dough forms. If necessary, stir in additional baking mix or yogurt to make dough easy to handle. Divide dough into 6 pieces and drop onto a lightly floured surface. With floured hands, shape each piece into a ball. Place in pan.
3. Bake 15 to 20 minutes or until light brown.

MINCEMEAT SCONES   6 scones

1 3/4 to 2 cups baking mix
3/4 cup mincemeat
2 tablespoons dark rum
2 tablespoons milk
2 tablespoons sugar

1. Heat oven to 450°. Spray an 8-inch round cake pan with nonstick cooking spray.
2. Mix 1 3/4 cups baking mix and remaining ingredients until soft dough forms. If dough is too sticky, gradually stir in enough baking mix (up to 1/4 cup) to make dough easy to handle. Divide dough into 6 pieces and drop onto a lightly floured surface. With floured hands, shape each piece into a ball. Place in pan.
3. Bake 15 to 20 minutes or until golden brown.

PINEAPPLE-COCONUT MUFFINS   12 muffins

2 cups baking mix
1/2 cup sugar
1/2 cup flaked coconut
1/2 cup milk
1 can (8 1/4 ounces) crushed pineapple in syrup
1 egg
2 tablespoons vegetable oil
1 teaspoon imitation coconut extract
1/2 teaspoon vanilla extract

1. Heat oven to 400°. Line 12 medium muffin cups, 2 1/2 x 1 1/4 inches, with paper baking cups.
2. Mix baking mix, sugar, and coconut in large bowl. Beat milk, pineapple, egg, oil, coconut extract, and vanilla in small bowl. Stir milk mixture into baking mix mixture just until moistened. Divide batter evenly among muffin cups.
3. Bake 20 to 25 minutes or until light brown. Serve warm or cool.

ITALIAN BEER MUFFINS   12 muffins

3 cups baking mix
1/2 cup grated Parmesan cheese
1/4 cup sugar
1 tablespoon dried minced onion
2 teaspoons minced garlic
1/2 teaspoon coarse black pepper
1/4 teaspoon salt
1 can (12 ounces) beer (1 1/2 cups)

1. Heat oven to 425°. Spray 12 medium muffin cups, 2 1/2 x 1 1/4 inches, with nonstick cooking spray.
2. Mix baking mix, Parmesan cheese, sugar, dried minced onion, garlic, pepper, and salt in large bowl. Stir beer into baking mix mixture just until moistened. Divide batter evenly among muffin cups.
3. Bake 15 to 20 minutes or until light brown. Loosen muffins from pan; remove from pan. Serve warm or cool.

GERMAN BEER MUFFINS: Omit garlic. Add 2 teaspoons caraway seed to baking mix mixture.

PEANUT BUTTER BREAD   1 loaf

3/4 cup crunchy or creamy peanut butter
3/4 cup sugar
1 cup milk
1 egg
1 teaspoon vanilla extract
2 cups flour
2 teaspoons baking powder
1 teaspoon salt

1. Heat oven to 350°. Spray an 8 1/2-inch loaf dish with nonstick cooking spray; lightly flour.
2. Beat peanut butter and sugar in large bowl with electric mixer on low speed. Gradually beat in milk. Beat in egg and vanilla on low speed. Mix

flour, baking powder, and salt in small bowl. Stir flour mixture into peanut butter mixture just until moistened. Pour into dish.

3. Bake 45 to 50 minutes or until toothpick inserted in center comes out almost clean (moist crumb). Cool 10 minutes in dish on wire rack. Loosen side of loaf from dish; remove from dish and place top side up on wire rack. Cool completely before slicing. Serve with jam or preserves.

HUMMINGBIRD BREAD   1 loaf

1/2 cup vegetable oil
1 cup sugar
2 eggs
1 cup mashed banana
1 can (8 1/4 ounces) crushed pineapple in syrup, drained with syrup reserved (firmly press pineapple to remove syrup)
3 tablespoons reserved pineapple syrup
1 can (3 1/2 ounces) flaked coconut
1 tablespoon imitation coconut extract
2 cups flour
1 teaspoon baking soda
1/2 teaspoon baking powder
1/2 teaspoon salt
1 1/4 teaspoons ground cinnamon
1/2 cup chopped pecans

1. Heat oven to 350°. Spray an 8 1/2-inch loaf dish with nonstick cooking spray; lightly flour.

2. Mix oil and sugar in large bowl. Stir in eggs and banana. Stir in crushed pineapple, 3 tablespoons pineapple syrup, coconut, and coconut extract. Mix flour, baking soda, baking powder, salt, and cinnamon in small bowl. Stir flour mixture into banana mixture just until moistened. Stir in pecans. Pour into dish.

3. Bake 1 hour to 1 hour 5 minutes or until toothpick inserted in center comes out clean. Cool 10 minutes in dish on wire rack. Loosen side of loaf from dish; remove from dish and place top side up on wire rack. Cool completely before slicing. Serve with cream cheese.

TOFFEE BREAD   1 loaf

1/2 cup margarine, melted
3/4 cup packed light brown sugar
1/4 cup sugar
1 egg
2 teaspoons imitation maple extract
2 1/4 cups flour
1 tablespoon baking powder
1/2 teaspoon salt
1 cup plus 2 tablespoons milk
1 cup almond toffee bits or English toffee bits
1 teaspoon flour
Garnish: 1/4 cup almond toffee bits or English toffee bits

1. Heat oven to 350°. Grease an 8 1/2-inch loaf dish with shortening; lightly flour.
2. Beat margarine, brown sugar, sugar, egg, and maple extract in large bowl with electric mixer on low speed. Mix flour, baking powder, and salt in small bowl. Beat flour mixture and milk alternately into sugar mixture on low speed.
3. Toss 1 cup almond toffee bits and 1 teaspoon flour. Stir in almond toffee bits mixture. Pour into dish. Sprinkle with 1/4 cup almond toffee bits.
4. Bake 55 to 60 minutes or until toothpick inserted in center comes out clean. Cool 10 minutes in dish on wire rack. Loosen side of loaf from dish; remove from dish and place top side up on wire rack. Cool completely before slicing.

PRALINE BREAD:

1. Substitute 1 cup chopped toasted pecans* for the almond toffee bits.
2. Omit almond toffee bit garnish. Substitute garnish: Mix 1/3 cup packed light brown sugar and 1 tablespoon cold margarine, cut into small pieces, with fork until crumbly. Stir in 1/4 cup chopped toasted pecans. Sprinkle mixture over batter. Bake as directed.

*TOASTED PECANS

Heat oven to 300°. Place 1 1/4 cups chopped pecans in single layer in shallow baking pan. Bake 20 minutes, stirring once. Cool to room temperature.

BLACK FOREST BREAD   1 loaf

1/2 cup butter, softened
1 cup plus 2 tablespoons sugar
1 egg
1 teaspoon vanilla extract
2 cups sifted flour
1/4 cup unsweetened cocoa powder
1 teaspoon baking soda
1 teaspoon ground cinnamon
3/4 teaspoon salt
1/8 teaspoon ground nutmeg
1 cup sour milk
2 tablespoons dark rum
1/2 cup dried cranberries
Drizzle: 2 tablespoons dark rum

1. Heat oven to 350°. Grease an 8 1/2-inch loaf dish with shortening; lightly flour.
2. Beat butter and sugar in large bowl with electric mixer on low speed. Beat in egg and vanilla. Sift together flour, cocoa, baking soda, cinnamon, salt, and nutmeg in small bowl. Beat flour mixture, milk, and 2 tablespoons dark rum alternately into sugar mixture on low speed. Stir in dried cranberries. Pour into dish.
3. Bake 55 to 60 minutes or until toothpick inserted in center comes out clean. Puncture top of loaf with skewer or fork; drizzle with 2 tablespoons dark rum. Cool 10 minutes in dish on wire rack. Loosen side of loaf from dish; remove from dish and place top side up on wire rack. Cool completely before slicing. Serve with cream cheese.

BUTTERSCOTCH-APPLE COFFEE CAKE

9 servings

2 cups baking mix
1 cup butterscotch chips, melted
1 cup chopped apple
1/2 cup milk
1 egg
1/2 teaspoon ground cinnamon
1 teaspoon vanilla extract
Topping:
1/2 cup baking mix
1/3 cup packed light brown sugar
2 1/2 tablespoons cold margarine, cut into small pieces
1 teaspoon ground cinnamon
Garnish: 1/2 cup butterscotch chips

1. Heat oven to 400°. Spray a 9-inch square baking pan with nonstick cooking spray.
2. Mix baking mix, melted butterscotch chips, apple, milk, egg, cinnamon, and vanilla in large mixing bowl until combined. Spread in pan.
3. Mix all topping ingredients with fork until crumbly. Sprinkle topping over batter; sprinkle butterscotch chips over topping.
4. Bake 25 to 30 minutes or until toothpick inserted in center comes out clean. Cool in pan on wire rack.

BLUEBERRY CHEESECAKE COFFEE CAKE

9 servings

1 can (16 1/2 ounces) blueberries in syrup, drained with syrup reserved
2/3 cup reserved blueberry syrup
2 cups baking mix
1/4 cup sugar
1 egg
1/2 teaspoon vanilla extract
1/2 teaspoon almond extract
2 tablespoons flour
1 package (8 ounces) cream cheese, cut into 1/2-inch cubes
Topping:
1/3 cup baking mix

1/3 cup packed light brown sugar
2 tablespoons cold margarine, cut into small pieces

1. Heat oven to 400°. Spray a 9-inch square baking pan with nonstick cooking spray; lightly flour.
2. Drain blueberries, reserving 2/3 cup syrup. Set aside blueberries.
3. Mix 2/3 cup blueberry syrup, baking mix, sugar, egg, vanilla, and almond extract until combined. Toss blueberries and 2 tablespoons flour; gently fold blueberry-flour mixture and cream cheese cubes into baking mix mixture. Spread in pan.
4. Mix all topping ingredients with fork until crumbly. Sprinkle over batter.
5. Bake 25 to 30 minutes. Cool in pan on wire rack. Refrigerate any remaining coffee cake.

PUMPKIN COFFEE CAKE   9 servings

2 cups baking mix
1/2 cup sugar
1 teaspoon ground cinnamon
1/4 teaspoon ground ginger
1/4 teaspoon ground nutmeg
1/2 cup canned pumpkin
1 egg
1/4 cup sour cream
2 tablespoons butter, melted
1 teaspoon imitation maple extract
Topping:
1/3 cup flour
3 tablespoons packed light brown sugar
1 teaspoon ground cinnamon
3 tablespoons cold butter, cut into small pieces

1. Heat oven to 450°. Spray an 8-inch square baking pan or a 9-inch round cake pan with nonstick cooking spray.
2. Mix baking mix, sugar, cinnamon, ginger, and nutmeg in large bowl. Stir in pumpkin, egg, sour cream, butter, and maple extract until combined. Spread in pan.
3. Mix all topping ingredients with fork until crumbly. Sprinkle over batter.
4. Bake 15 to 20 minutes or until toothpick inserted in center comes out almost clean (moist crumb). Cool in pan on wire rack.

CHRISTMAS COFFEE CAKE   9 servings

Coffee Cake:
2 cups baking mix
1 cup mincemeat
1/2 cup milk
1/2 cup mixed candied fruit, chopped
1/2 cup chopped pecans or walnuts
1/4 cup sugar
1 egg
2 tablespoons dark rum
Topping:
1/2 cup baking mix
1/3 cup packed light brown sugar
2 tablespoons cold margarine, cut into small pieces
Drizzle: 1/4 cup dark rum
Vanilla Glaze (below)
Garnish: Maraschino cherries with stem, drained

1. Heat oven to 425°. Spray a 9-inch square baking pan with nonstick cooking spray.
2. Mix all coffee cake ingredients in large bowl until combined. Spread in pan.
3. Mix all topping ingredients with fork until crumbly. Sprinkle topping over batter.
4. Bake 20 to 25 minutes or until toothpick inserted in center comes out almost clean (moist crumb). Drizzle with rum. Cool in pan on wire rack.
5. Drizzle with Vanilla Glaze. Garnish with maraschino cherries.

VANILLA GLAZE

2/3 cup powdered sugar
2 to 3 teaspoons milk
1/4 teaspoon vanilla extract

Mix all ingredients until smooth and thin enough to drizzle.

CHOCOLATE CHIP COFFEE CAKE   9 servings

1 1/2 cups baking mix
1/2 cup sugar
1/3 cup plus 1 1/2 tablespoons milk
1 egg
2 tablespoons butter, softened
1 teaspoon imitation maple extract
1/2 teaspoon imitation coconut extract
3/4 cup miniature semisweet chocolate chips
1 teaspoon flour
Topping:
1/3 cup flour
1/3 cup packed light brown sugar
3 tablespoons cold butter, cut into small pieces
Garnish: 1/2 cup miniature semisweet chocolate chips

1. Heat oven to 350°. Line a 9-inch square baking pan with aluminum foil. Grease with shortening; lightly flour.
2. Beat baking mix, sugar, milk, egg, butter, maple extract, and coconut extract with electric mixer on medium speed 2 minutes. Toss 3/4 cup miniature chocolate chips and 1 teaspoon flour; stir in chocolate chip mixture. Spread in pan.
3. Mix all topping ingredients with fork until crumbly; sprinkle over batter. Sprinkle 1/2 miniature chocolate chips over topping.
4. Bake 25 to 30 minutes or until toothpick inserted in center comes out clean (cake surface is irregular). Cool in pan on wire rack.
5. Lift coffee cake out of pan with aluminum foil. Cut into squares; remove from aluminum foil with spatula.

CINNAMON CHIP COFFEE CAKE

Coffee cake: Increase milk to 1/3 cup plus 2 tablespoons. Omit maple extract and coconut extract. Add 1 teaspoon vanilla extract and 1 tablespoon ground cinnamon. Substitute 3/4 cup cinnamon chips for miniature semisweet chocolate chips.
Topping: Add 1/2 teaspoon ground cinnamon.
Garnish: Substitute 1/2 cup cinnamon chips for miniature semisweet chocolate chips.

CORN BREAD WAFFLES   3 to 4 waffles

1 1/2 cups flour
1/2 cup yellow cornmeal
2 tablespoons sugar
1 tablespoon baking powder
1/2 teaspoon salt
1 1/3 cups milk
1 egg
6 tablespoons margarine, melted
Serve with: Maple syrup for breakfast or chili for lunch or dinner

1. Heat waffle iron.
2. Beat all ingredients until well blended. Pour a scant 2/3 cup batter onto center of hot waffle iron; close iron.
3. Bake until steaming stops and waffle is golden brown. Carefully remove waffle. Repeat with remaining batter.

OAT-NUT PANCAKES   4 pancakes

1 cup baking mix
1/4 cup oat bran cereal, uncooked
1/4 cup chopped pecans or walnuts
1 tablespoon wheat germ
2/3 cup milk
1 egg
1 tablespoon vegetable oil
1 teaspoon vanilla extract
Vegetable oil or shortening (for griddle)
Maple-Butter Syrup:
1/2 cup maple syrup
1/4 cup butter, cut into pieces

1. Mix baking mix, oat bran cereal, nuts, and wheat germ. Beat in milk, egg, oil, and vanilla until blended.
2. Heat oil in griddle over medium-high heat. Pour batter by scant 1/4 cupfuls onto hot griddle. Reduce heat to medium. Cook until pancakes are puffed and dry around edges. Turn; cook until light brown.

3. While pancakes are cooking, prepare syrup. Heat maple syrup and butter in small saucepan over medium heat until hot and butter is melted. Serve syrup over pancakes.

GINGERBREAD PANCAKES   4 pancakes

1 cup baking mix
1/2 teaspoon ground cinnamon
1/4 teaspoon ground ginger
1/8 teaspoon ground cloves
1/3 cup milk
2 tablespoons molasses
1 tablespoon vegetable oil
1 egg
Vegetable oil or shortening (for griddle)
Lemon-Maple Syrup:
1/2 cup maple syrup
2 teaspoons lemon juice
Serve with: Cream cheese, softened

1. Mix baking mix, cinnamon, ginger, and cloves in medium bowl. Stir milk, molasses, oil, and egg in measuring cup. Beat in milk mixture until blended.
2. Heat oil in griddle over medium-high heat. Pour batter by scant 1/4 cupfuls onto hot griddle. Reduce heat to medium-low. Cook until pancakes are puffed and dry around edges. Turn; cook until light brown.
3. While pancakes are cooking, prepare syrup. Heat maple syrup and lemon juice until hot. Keep warm.
4. Spread softened cream cheese on pancake. Pour warm syrup over cream cheese.

CARIBBEAN PANCAKES   4 pancakes

1 cup baking mix
1/2 cup milk
1/2 cup flaked coconut
1 egg
1 tablespoon white rum
1/2 teaspoon ground cinnamon
Vegetable oil or shortening (for griddle)
1 medium banana, sliced
Rum-Maple Syrup:
1/2 cup maple syrup
2 teaspoons white rum

1. Mix baking mix, milk, coconut, egg, rum, and cinnamon until blended.
2. Heat oil in griddle over medium-high heat. Pour batter by scant 1/4
cupfuls onto hot griddle. Reduce heat to medium. Place banana slices on
each pancake spacing evenly. Cook until pancakes are puffed and dry around
edges. Turn; cook until light brown.
3. While pancakes are cooking, heat maple syrup until hot. Stir in rum. Serve
syrup over pancakes.

PUMPKIN PANCAKES   4 to 6 pancakes

1 cup baking mix
1 can (5 ounces) evaporated milk (about 2/3 cup)
1 egg
1/2 cup canned pumpkin
1 teaspoon ground cinnamon
1/4 teaspoon ground nutmeg
1/4 teaspoon ground ginger
Vegetable oil or shortening (for griddle)
Serve with: Maple syrup

1. Mix all ingredients except oil until blended.
2. Heat oil in griddle over medium-high heat. Pour batter by scant 1/4
cupfuls onto hot griddle. Reduce heat to medium. Cook until pancakes are
puffed and dry around edges. Turn; cook until light brown.

FLORIDA SUNSHINE TOAST   4 slices toast

Orange Syrup (below)
2 eggs
1/2 cup orange juice
2 tablespoons sugar
1/4 teaspoon almond extract, scant
1 to 2 tablespoons butter
4 slices bread
MENU: Sausage

1. Prepare Orange Syrup; keep warm.
2. Beat eggs, orange juice, sugar, and almond extract until foamy.
3. Melt butter in large skillet or griddle over medium-low heat.
4. Dip bread into egg mixture; place in skillet. Cook about 3 minutes on each side or until brown. Watch carefully! The toast will burn if the heat is too high. Serve with warm syrup.

ORANGE SYRUP   about 1/2 cup

1/4 cup butter
1/4 cup orange juice
2 tablespoons sugar
1/4 teaspoon grated orange peel
1 teaspoon cornstarch

1. Melt butter in small saucepan over medium heat. Stir in orange juice, sugar, and orange peel. Heat to boiling; boil 1 minute. Reduce heat to medium.
2. Mix cornstarch with 2 tablespoons of orange juice mixture. Stir cornstarch mixture into orange juice mixture. Cook, stirring constantly, until thickened.

CORN BREAD   9 servings

1 tablespoon margarine
1 cup yellow cornmeal
1 cup flour
2 tablespoons sugar
2 1/2 teaspoons baking powder
3/4 teaspoon salt
1 cup milk
1 egg
1/4 cup vegetable oil

1. Heat oven to 450°. Grease an 8-inch square baking dish with 1 tablespoon margarine.
2. Stir together cornmeal, flour, sugar, baking powder, and salt in large bowl. Beat milk, egg, and oil in small bowl. Stir milk mixture into cornmeal mixture just until moistened. Pour batter into dish.
3. Bake 15 to 18 minutes or until light brown and toothpick inserted in center comes out clean. Serve warm or cool.

CARAWAY CORN BREAD: Add 2 teaspoons caraway seeds to cornmeal mixture.

HERB CORN BREAD: Add 1 teaspoon dried thyme leaves, 1 teaspoon dried chives, 1/4 teaspoon garlic powder, 1/4 teaspoon coarse black pepper, and 1 teaspoon minced garlic to cornmeal mixture.

LEMON CORN BREAD: Add 2 teaspoons grated lemon peel to cornmeal mixture. Serve cool.

NEW MEXICAN CORN BREAD: Add 8 slices turkey bacon, crisply cooked and crumbled, 1/3 cup chopped green onions, 1/3 cup chopped red bell pepper, 1 teaspoon ground cumin, 1/2 teaspoon rubbed sage, and 1/4 teaspoon coarse black pepper to cornmeal mixture. Refrigerate any remaining corn bread.

PARMESAN CORN BREAD: Add 2/3 cup grated Parmesan cheese to cornmeal mixture. After spreading batter into dish, sprinkle with 2 tablespoons Parmesan cheese.

BANANA CORN BREAD   9 servings

1 tablespoon margarine
1 cup yellow cornmeal
1 cup flour
1/4 cup sugar
2 teaspoons baking powder
1/2 teaspoon baking soda
3/4 teaspoon salt
1 cup milk
1 egg
1/2 cup mashed banana
1/4 cup vegetable oil
1/2 cup chopped banana

1. Heat oven to 450°. Grease an 8-inch square baking dish with 1 tablespoon margarine.
2. Stir together cornmeal, flour, sugar, baking powder, baking soda, and salt in large bowl. Beat milk, egg, mashed banana, and oil in small bowl. Stir milk mixture and chopped banana into cornmeal mixture just until moistened. Pour batter into dish.
3. Bake 20 to 25 minutes or until golden brown and toothpick inserted in center comes out clean.

HONEY CORN BREAD   6 servings

1 cup plus 2 tablespoons baking mix
1/2 cup yellow cornmeal
1/2 cup milk
2 tablespoons honey
1 egg
Garnish: 1 tablespoon butter

1. Heat oven to 400°. Spray an 8-inch round cake pan with nonstick cooking spray.
2. Stir together baking mix and cornmeal in medium bowl. Mix milk, honey, and egg in liquid measuring cup. Stir milk mixture into baking mix mixture just until moistened. Pour batter into pan.
3. Bake 15 to 20 minutes or until lightly browned. Remove from oven. Immediately rub 1 tablespoon butter over top of corn bread.

PARMESAN-GARLIC BREADSTICKS

10 breadsticks

1 cup baking mix
1/4 cup grated Parmesan cheese
1/4 cup cold water
1 teaspoon minced garlic
1/4 teaspoon coarse black pepper
Butter

1. Heat oven to 425°. Line a baking sheet with aluminum foil.
2. Mix all ingredients except butter in medium bowl. Turn dough onto surface dusted with baking mix; gently roll to coat. Shape into ball; knead 5 times. Roll dough into 5x10-inch rectangle. Cut lengthwise into five 1-inch strips; cut each strip in half. Place on baking sheet.
3. Bake 10 to 15 minutes or until golden brown. Brush hot breadsticks with butter. Serve warm or cool.

ONION PAN BREAD

6 servings

1 1/2 cups baking mix
3 tablespoons dried minced onion
2 tablespoons grated Parmesan cheese
1/4 teaspoon coarse black pepper
1/4 cup milk
1 egg
2 tablespoons butter, melted
1 tablespoon grated Parmesan cheese

1. Heat oven to 400°. Spray an 8-inch round cake pan with nonstick cooking spray.
2. Mix baking mix, onion, Parmesan cheese, and pepper. Beat in milk and egg until combined. Spread batter into a 7-inch circle in pan. Drizzle with butter and sprinkle with Parmesan cheese.
3. Bake 20 to 25 minutes or until light brown. Serve warm.

FLOUR TORTILLAS   8 tortillas

1 1/2 cups baking mix
1/2 cup flour
3/4 teaspoon baking powder
2 tablespoons shortening
1/2 to 3/4 cup water
Additional baking mix and flour, if needed

1. Mix baking mix, flour, and baking powder in medium bowl. Cut in shortening with fork until crumbly. Gradually stir in water until soft dough forms. If dough is too sticky, gradually stir in equal amounts of baking mix and flour (start with 1/2 tablespoon each) to make dough easy to handle.
2. Turn dough onto lightly floured surface; gently roll to coat. Shape into ball; knead 2 minutes or until smooth. Divide dough into 8 pieces; roll each piece into a ball. Flatten ball in your hand. Place on lightly floured surface and roll into a 6- to 7-inch circle. Dough should be very thin. Repeat with remaining dough.
3. Heat an ungreased griddle over medium-high heat. Place 2 tortillas in griddle; cook over medium-high heat until surface of tortillas start to bubble. The underside of the tortilla will be brown in spots. Turn; cook until underside of tortilla is brown in spots.
4. Stack cooked tortillas on paper towel and cover with damp dish towel. Carefully wipe flour off griddle; repeat with remaining dough.

WHEAT TORTILLAS: Reduce flour to 1/4 cup. Add 1/4 cup whole wheat flour to baking mix mixture.

BAKED CORN TORTILLA STRIPS   2 servings

4 corn tortillas (5 to 6 inches in diameter)
Salt
Serve with: Soup or chili

1. Heat oven to 425°. Line a shallow baking pan with aluminum foil.
2. Stack tortillas and cut crosswise into 1-inch strips. Place in single layer in pan. Sprinkle with salt.
3. Bake 10 minutes. Loosen strips with spatula and check crispness. Bake 2 to 3 minutes longer if crisper strips are desired.

GREEK PIZZETTES   5 pizzettes

1 package (10.2 ounces) refrigerated large buttermilk biscuits
  (5 biscuits)
Flour
Toppings:
1/2 cup crumbled feta cheese (2 ounces)
1 large clove garlic, minced
1/2 cup sliced black olives
2 teaspoons capers, drained
1 teaspoon dried thyme leaves
1/4 teaspoon coarse black pepper

1. Heat oven to 400°. Line a shallow baking pan with aluminum foil and
spray with nonstick cooking spray.
2. Roll each biscuit into a 4 1/2-inch circle on lightly floured surface. Place
in pan. Bake 3 minutes or until set.
3. Arrange toppings in order listed on crust. Bake 12 to 15 minutes longer or
until light brown.

ITALIAN PIZZETTES: In Step #3 substitute the following toppings,
dividing evenly among 5 pizzettes. Spread crusts with 1/4 cup tomato paste.
Sprinkle with 1 teaspoon dried basil leaves, 1/2 teaspoon dried oregano
leaves, and 1 large clove garlic, minced. Top with 1 1/2 ounces sliced
pepperoni (about 24 slices) and 1/4 cup chopped black olives. Sprinkle with
1 cup shredded mozzarella cheese (4 ounces) and 2 tablespoons grated
Parmesan cheese.

FRENCH PIZZETTES: In Step #3 substitute the following toppings,
dividing evenly among 5 pizzettes. Spread crusts with 6 tablespoons whole
berry cranberry sauce. Sprinkle with 4 ounces Brie cheese, cut into cubes
(1 cup), and 2 tablespoons chopped pecans.

FRENCH-STYLE PIZZA   8 servings

1 can (8 ounces) refrigerated crescent rolls (8 rolls)
Toppings:
2 tablespoons tomato paste
1 teaspoon dried parsley flakes
1 teaspoon dried oregano leaves
1 teaspoon dried basil leaves
2 large cloves garlic, minced
3/4 cup cubed fully cooked ham
1 cup sliced mushrooms (3 ounces)
1/2 medium red bell pepper, cut into 1/4-inch strips
Salt and pepper
1/4 cup grated Parmesan cheese
5 ounces shredded mozzarella cheese (1 1/4 cups)

1. Heat oven to 375°. Spray a 12-inch pizza pan with nonstick cooking spray.
2. Separate dough into 8 triangles. Place in pizza pan; press over bottom and up side to form crust. Bake 5 minutes or until set.
3. Spread tomato paste evenly over crust. Sprinkle with parsley, oregano, basil, and garlic. Top with ham, sliced mushrooms, and pepper strips. Sprinkle with salt, pepper, and Parmesan cheese.
4. Bake 12 to 15 minutes or until crust is light brown. Sprinkle with mozzarella cheese. Bake 3 to 5 minutes longer or until cheese is melted.

FRENCH BREAD WITH SOUTHWESTERN BUTTER

Spread sliced French bread with a Southwestern Butter (page 138). Broil until brown.

ITALIAN SAUSAGE-PEPPER PIZZA

8 servings

Pizza Crust:
1 teaspoon regular or quick active dry yeast
1 teaspoon sugar
3/4 cup warm water (110°)
3/4 teaspoon salt
1 tablespoon vegetable oil
2 cups flour*
Toppings:
1/3 cup tomato paste
1 teaspoon dried oregano leaves
1 teaspoon dried basil leaves
1 large clove garlic, minced
1/4 pound cooked Italian Meatballs (page 106), crumbled (1 cup)
   or 1/4 pound cooked turkey sausage, crumbled (1 cup)
1/2 cup halved black olives
1/2 red bell pepper, cut into 1/4-inch strips
Salt and pepper
1 tablespoon vegetable oil
3 tablespoons grated Parmesan cheese
4 ounces shredded mozzarella cheese (1 cup)

SHORTCUT:
Substitute refrigerated pizza dough or prebaked pizza crust for homemade pizza crust. Follow directions listed on the package.

1. Dissolve yeast and sugar in warm water in liquid measuring cup. Stir in salt and oil. Pour into medium bowl. Vigorously stir in flour, stirring until soft dough forms. Cover bowl with plastic wrap; let rise in warm place 5 minutes (dough will not be doubled).
2. Heat oven to 425°. Generously grease a 12-inch pizza pan with shortening. Grease hands with shortening; press dough into pan. Bake 5 to 7 minutes or until set.
3. Increase oven temperature to 450°. Spread tomato paste evenly over crust. Sprinkle remaining topping ingredients except mozzarella cheese over tomato paste in order listed. Bake 15 to 20 minutes or until crust is light brown. Sprinkle with mozzarella cheese. Bake 3 to 5 minutes longer or until cheese is melted.
* For **WHEAT CRUST:** Reduce flour to 1 1/2 cups. Add 1/2 cup whole wheat flour with the flour.

MEXICAN SAUSAGE-PEPPER PIZZA: Substitute 1 teaspoon chili powder and 1 teaspoon ground cumin for oregano and basil. Substitute 1/2 cup chopped green bell pepper for red bell pepper strips. Substitute 4 ounces shredded Monterey Jack cheese (1 cup) for mozzarella cheese.

VEGETARIAN MEXICAN PIZZA   8 servings

Pizza Crust:
1 teaspoon regular or quick active dry yeast
1 teaspoon sugar
3/4 cup warm water (110°)
3/4 teaspoon salt
1/2 teaspoon coarse black pepper
1 tablespoon vegetable oil
2 cups flour

SHORTCUT:
Substitute refrigerated pizza dough or prebaked pizza crust for homemade pizza crust. Follow directions listed on the package.

Toppings:
3 tablespoons tomato paste
3 tablespoons strained picante sauce
1/3 cup sliced black olives
1 large clove garlic, minced
Salt and pepper
1 tablespoon vegetable oil
4 ounces shredded Monterey Jack cheese (1 cup)
Garnish: 1 teaspoon dried parsley flakes

1. Dissolve yeast and sugar in warm water in liquid measuring cup. Stir in salt, pepper, and oil. Pour into medium bowl. Vigorously stir in flour, stirring until soft dough forms. Cover bowl with plastic wrap; let rise in warm place 5 minutes (dough will not be doubled).
2. Heat oven to 425°. Generously grease a 12-inch pizza pan with shortening. Grease hands with shortening; press dough into pan. Bake 5 to 7 minutes or until set.
3. Increase oven temperature to 450°. Mix tomato paste and strained picante sauce; spread evenly over crust. Sprinkle remaining topping ingredients except cheese over tomato paste in order listed. Bake 15 to 20 minutes or until crust is light brown. Sprinkle with cheese. Bake 3 to 5 minutes longer or until cheese is melted. Sprinkle with parsley.

FOCACCIA   8 servings

1 teaspoon quick active dry yeast
1 teaspoon sugar
3/4 cup warm water (110°)
2 tablespoons olive oil, divided
3/4 teaspoon salt
2 cups flour
2 teaspoons dried rosemary leaves
2 teaspoons minced garlic
1/2 teaspoon coarse black pepper

1. Dissolve yeast and sugar in warm water in liquid measuring cup. Stir
in 1 tablespoon olive oil and salt. Pour into medium bowl. Vigorously stir in
flour, rosemary, garlic, and pepper, stirring until soft dough forms. Cover
bowl with plastic wrap; let rise in warm place 10 minutes (dough will not be
doubled).
2. Set oven to 425°. Generously grease a 12-inch pizza pan with shortening.
Grease hands with shortening; press dough into pan. Place pan in oven
(temperature will not have reached 425°).
3. Bake 15 minutes. Drizzle bread with remaining 1 tablespoon olive oil.
Bake 5 minutes longer or until brown.

HERB FOCACCIA: Substitute 2 tablespoons vegetable oil for olive oil.
Omit rosemary and garlic. Add 2 teaspoons dried chives and 1 teaspoon
dried dill weed.

ITALIAN HERB FOCACCIA: Substitute 2 tablespoons vegetable oil
for olive oil. Omit rosemary. Add 1/4 cup Parmesan cheese, 1 teaspoon dried
basil leaves, and 1 teaspoon dried oregano leaves.

ONION FOCACCIA: Substitute 2 tablespoons vegetable oil for olive oil.
Omit rosemary and garlic. Add 1 tablespoon dried minced onion.

SOUTHWESTERN FOCACCIA: Substitute 2 tablespoons vegetable
oil for olive oil. Omit rosemary. Reduce minced garlic to 1/2 teaspoon. Add
1 teaspoon chili powder and 1 teaspoon ground cumin.

PESTO-TOPPED FOCACCIA   **8 servings**

1 teaspoon quick active dry yeast
1 teaspoon sugar
3/4 cup warm water (110°)
1 tablespoon vegetable oil
3/4 teaspoon salt
2 cups flour
1/2 teaspoon coarse black pepper
1/4 to 1/3 cup pesto

SHORTCUT:
Substitute refrigerated pizza
dough or prebaked pizza crust
for homemade focaccia. Follow
directions listed on the package.

1. Dissolve yeast and sugar in warm water in liquid measuring cup. Stir in oil
and salt. Pour into medium bowl. Vigorously stir in flour and pepper, stirring
until soft dough forms. Cover bowl with plastic wrap; let rise in warm
place 10 minutes (dough will not be doubled).
2. Set oven to 425°. Generously grease a 12-inch pizza pan with shortening.
Grease hands with shortening; press dough into pan. Place pan in oven
(temperature will not have reached 425°).
3. Bake 17 minutes. Spread pesto over dough. Use the back of a spoon to
spread the pesto as evenly as possible. Bake 5 minutes longer or until crust is
brown. Refrigerate any remaining bread.

COILED BREAD   **1 loaf**

1. Prepare Rosemary Bread or Thyme Bread (page 46) through Step #3.
2. Grease a 9-inch round cake pan with shortening.
3. Punch down dough. Roll dough into a 10x17-inch rectangle on lightly
floured surface. Roll up from long side. Curl dough into a coil shape, tucking
end under loaf. Place in pan. Loosely cover with plastic wrap and let rise in
warm place 30 minutes or until double.
4. Heat oven to 425°. Bake 25 to 30 minutes or until loaf is brown and
sounds hollow when tapped. Serve warm or cool.

ROSEMARY BREAD   1 loaf

1 tablespoon quick active dry yeast
1 tablespoon sugar
1 cup warm water (110°)
3 cups flour
2 tablespoons shortening
1 1/2 teaspoons salt
1 1/2 teaspoons dried rosemary leaves
1 teaspoon dried parsley leaves
1/4 teaspoon dried thyme leaves

1. Dissolve yeast and sugar in warm water in liquid measuring cup; let stand 5 to 10 minutes or until foamy.
2. Mix flour, shortening, salt, rosemary, parsley, and thyme in food processor. Add yeast mixture; process 5 seconds or until dough forms a ball (dough should be smooth). If dough is too sticky, gradually add flour (1 tablespoon at a time); process until blended. If dough is too dry, gradually add water (1 tablespoon at a time); process until blended. Process 30 to 45 seconds to knead.
3. Spray a large bowl with nonstick cooking spray. Place dough in bowl; turn to coat. Loosely cover bowl with plastic wrap. Let rise in warm place about 30 minutes or until double.
4. Grease a baking sheet with shortening.
5. Punch down dough. Roll dough into a 10x17-inch rectangle on lightly floured surface. Roll up from long side. Pinch ends together and tuck under loaf. Place loaf on baking sheet. Slash top of loaf. Loosely cover with plastic wrap and let rise in warm place 30 minutes or until double.
6. Heat oven to 400°. Spray loaf with water. Bake 30 minutes or until loaf is brown and sounds hollow when tapped. Serve warm or cool.

THYME BREAD: Omit rosemary and parsley. Increase dried thyme leaves to 1 1/2 teaspoons and add 1/2 teaspoon coarse black pepper. Knead in 1 teaspoon minced garlic by hand on lightly floured surface after kneading dough in food processor.

OAT BRAN ENGLISH MUFFIN BREAD   1 loaf

1 package (1/4 ounce) quick active dry yeast
1 teaspoon sugar
1/4 cup warm water (110°)
2 1/2 cups flour, divided
1/2 cup oat bran cereal, uncooked
1 1/4 teaspoons salt
1/8 teaspoon baking soda
1 cup warm water (110°)
White cornmeal
Garnish: Old-fashioned oats

1. Dissolve yeast and sugar in 1/4 cup warm water in liquid measuring cup; let stand 5 to 10 minutes or until foamy.
2. Mix 1 cup flour, oat bran cereal, salt, and baking soda in large bowl. Add yeast mixture and 1 cup warm water; stir until smooth. Stir in enough of remaining 1 1/2 cups flour to make dough easy to handle.
3. Turn dough onto lightly floured surface. Knead 1 minute. Grease an 8 1/2-inch loaf pan with shortening; sprinkle with white cornmeal. Shape dough into a loaf and place in pan. Spray one side of plastic wrap with nonstick cooking spray. Loosely cover pan with plastic wrap, sprayed side down. Let rise in warm place about 30 minutes or until double.
4. Heat oven to 400°. Spray loaf with water; sprinkle with oats. Bake 35 to 40 minutes or until loaf is brown and sounds hollow when tapped. Remove bread from pan and cool on wire rack. Slice and toast.

OATMEAL ENGLISH MUFFIN BREAD: Substitute 1/2 cup quick-cooking oats for 1/2 cup oat bran cereal.
CINNAMON-RAISIN ENGLISH MUFFIN BREAD: Stir in 3/4 cup raisins and 1 1/2 teaspoons ground cinnamon with yeast mixture and 1 cup water in Step #2. After placing dough in pan, sprinkle with mixture of 1 tablespoon sugar and 1/4 teaspoon ground cinnamon.
WHOLE WHEAT ENGLISH MUFFIN BREAD: Substitute 1/2 cup whole wheat flour for 1/2 cup oat bran cereal.

4

MAIN DISHES

For your convenience, all of the main dishes include a menu. Prepare the side dishes from scratch or save time by using convenience foods. The appetizing suggestions will make meal planning a snap.

BACON-TOMATO SPAGHETTI   2 servings

8 slices turkey bacon
2 tablespoons butter
1/2 cup chopped onion
1 teaspoon minced garlic
1 can (14 1/2 ounces) whole tomatoes
1 tablespoon tomato paste
1 teaspoon dried basil leaves
1 teaspoon dried parsley flakes
1/4 teaspoon salt
1/4 teaspoon coarse black pepper
2 to 4 tablespoons water, optional
MENU: Spaghetti, broccoli, and French bread

SHORTCUT:
For all of my recipes that use canned tomatoes, I prefer to chop canned whole tomatoes instead of using canned chopped tomatoes (I like large chunks of tomatoes). Save time by using canned chopped tomatoes, if desired.

1. Spray a large skillet with nonstick cooking spray. Fry bacon in cooking spray until brown and crisp. Drain. Crumble bacon into small pieces. Set aside.
2. Add butter to the skillet; melt over medium heat. Cook onion and garlic in butter until crisp-tender.
3. Coarsely chop tomatoes, reserving juice. Add tomatoes, tomato juice, crumbled bacon, and remaining ingredients except water to skillet; stir to combine. Heat to boiling; reduce heat to medium. Simmer uncovered 5 minutes, stirring occasionally. Thin sauce with water, if desired. Serve sauce over spaghetti.

DELI-STYLE ROAST BEEF   6 servings

3-pound beef sirloin tip roast
1 large clove garlic, cut into slivers
Salt and pepper
Dried thyme leaves
Dried marjoram leaves
Dried basil leaves
Condiment: Horseradish Sauce (below)
MENU: Macaroni-Olive Salad (page 130), tossed salad with salad
  dressing, and crusty rolls

1. Heat oven to 325°. Line a shallow baking pan with aluminum foil and spray with nonstick cooking spray.
2. Cut slits in beef using a sharp knife; insert garlic slivers. Sprinkle beef with salt, pepper, thyme, marjoram, and basil. Place in pan.
3. Roast uncovered 1 hour 15 minutes. Check temperature with instant-read thermometer. Continue to roast until instant-read thermometer reads 135° for medium-rare, 150° for medium, or until desired doneness is reached. Temperature will continue to rise about 5° after removing from oven.
4. Remove beef from oven. Cover roast loosely with tent of aluminum foil. Let stand 15 minutes for easiest carving.

HORSERADISH SAUCE   1 cup

1 package (8 ounces) cream cheese, softened
2 tablespoons cream style prepared horseradish
1 tablespoon sour cream

Beat all ingredients until smooth. Serve with beef.

OVEN-BARBECUED ROAST BEEF   4 servings

2-pound beef boneless round roast, cut into 2 equal pieces
Salt and pepper
1 cup ketchup
1/4 cup Worcestershire sauce
1/4 cup packed light brown sugar
1 tablespoon white vinegar
1 teaspoon dried oregano leaves
3/4 teaspoon garlic salt
1/2 teaspoon dried thyme leaves
MENU: Creamy Mashed Potatoes (page 145) and Herbed Bean Salad
   (page 124)

1. Heat oven to 325°. Line an 11x7x2-inch baking dish with aluminum
foil and spray with nonstick cooking spray.
2. Sprinkle beef with salt and pepper. Place in dish. Mix remaining
ingredients; pour over beef.
3. Cover dish tightly with aluminum foil and bake 3 hours. Carefully remove
foil allowing steam to escape. Let stand loosely covered 15 minutes before
serving.

SMOKY OVEN-BARBECUED ROAST BEEF: Add
1 1/2 teaspoons liquid smoke to ketchup mixture.

SLOW COOKER CARNE GUISADA   4 servings

2-pound beef boneless round roast, cut into 1 1/2-inch pieces (3 cups)
1 cup chopped green bell pepper
1 cup chopped onion
1 package (1 1/4 ounces) taco seasoning mix
1 can (14 1/2 ounces) whole tomatoes
2 beef bouillon cubes
1 to 2 tablespoons cornstarch, if desired
MENU: Rice, refried beans, tossed salad with salad dressing, and
   flour tortillas

1. Spray slow cooker and underside of lid with nonstick cooking spray.
2. Toss beef, green pepper, onion, and taco seasoning mix in large bowl. Place in slow cooker.
3. Coarsely chop tomatoes, reserving juice; place tomatoes in slow cooker on beef mixture. Place tomato juice and bouillon cubes in microwavable bowl. Heat on High (100%), stopping and stirring, until bouillon cubes are dissolved. Pour tomato juice mixture into slow cooker. Do not stir.
4. Cover and cook on low setting 8 to 9 hours. Do not remove lid during cooking process.
5. Thicken the stew, if desired. Mix about 1/2 cup of stew liquid with cornstarch. Stir in cornstarch mixture. Cook on high, stirring frequently, until thickened.

KENTUCKY-STYLE BARBECUED STEAK

4 servings

1 1/2-pound beef boneless sirloin steak
Salt and pepper
Kentucky Whiskey Barbecue Sauce:
Butter-flavored nonstick cooking spray
1/3 cup chopped onion
1 teaspoon minced garlic
1/3 cup ketchup
1/4 cup soy sauce
1/4 cup Kentucky whiskey
3 tablespoons honey
MENU: Mashed potatoes, Carrot-Zucchini Slaw (page 127) or
   purchased coleslaw, and toasted French bread

1. Trim excess fat from beef. Sprinkle with salt and pepper.
2. Heat grill. Grill beef uncovered 4 to 6 inches from medium heat 7 to 9 minutes for medium-rare or medium, turning once.
3. While beef is cooking, prepare sauce. Heat nonstick cooking spray over medium heat in saucepan. Cook onion and garlic in nonstick cooking spray, stirring frequently, until onion is crisp-tender. Add remaining sauce ingredients. Heat to boiling; boil 5 minutes, stirring occasionally. Sauce is thin. Serve beef with sauce.

ITALIAN HERBED STEAK   4 servings

1 1/2-pound beef boneless sirloin steak
1 tablespoon olive oil
2 teaspoons balsamic vinegar
1 large clove garlic, minced
1 teaspoon Italian seasoning
3/4 teaspoon salt
1/2 teaspoon coarse black pepper
MENU: Parmesan-Topped Potatoes (page 144) or baked potatoes with
    sour cream, and Italian-Style Tossed Salad (page 123) with salad
    dressing

1. Trim excess fat from beef. Mix olive oil, balsamic vinegar, garlic, Italian
seasoning, salt, and pepper. Spread mixture over beef. Let stand at room
temperature 15 minutes.
2. While beef is marinating, heat grill. Grill beef uncovered 4 to 6 inches
from medium heat 7 to 9 minutes for medium-rare or medium, turning once.

ZESTY STEAK   4 servings

1 1/2-pound beef boneless sirloin steak
4 teaspoons olive oil
3/4 teaspoon garlic powder
3/4 teaspoon lemon pepper
3/4 teaspoon salt
3/4 teaspoon coarse black pepper
MENU: Mushrooms and Onions (page 139) and tossed salad with
    salad dressing

1. Trim excess fat from beef. Mix olive oil, garlic powder, lemon pepper,
salt, and pepper. Spread mixture over beef.
2. Heat grill. Grill beef uncovered 4 to 6 inches from medium heat 7
to 9 minutes for medium-rare or medium, turning once.

TACO-FLAVORED BEEF KABOBS   4 servings

1 1/2-pound beef boneless sirloin steak
1 package (1 1/4 ounces) taco seasoning mix
1 large green bell pepper, cut into 1 1/2-inch pieces
1 large onion, cut into eighths
Condiments: Salsa, sour cream, and guacamole
MENU: Rice, Black Bean Salad (page 126), and Mexican Brownies
  (page 163)

1. Trim excess fat from beef. Cut beef into 1 1/2-inch pieces.
2. Place beef on ceramic or plastic plate. Coat beef with taco seasoning, tossing to coat.
3. Heat grill. While grill is heating, thread beef on 4 skewers, leaving space between each piece. Thread pepper and onion alternating on each of 4 skewers, leaving space between each piece.
4. Cover and grill vegetables 4 to 6 inches from medium heat 5 minutes. Turn vegetables. Add beef to grill. Cover and grill 5 to 7 minutes, turning beef once.

GRECIAN SKILLET STEAK   4 servings

1 1/2-pound beef boneless sirloin steak
Salt and pepper
Dried basil leaves
Dried oregano leaves
Garlic powder
MENU: Thyme Oven-Fried Potatoes (page 143), Greek Vegetable Salad
  (page 129), and pita bread

1. Trim excess fat from beef. Sprinkle with salt, pepper, basil, oregano, and garlic powder.
2. Heat grill pan until very hot. Brown beef on both sides, turning once. Reduce heat to medium; cook beef 6 to 8 minutes for medium-rare or medium, turning once.

ITALIAN BREADED PANFRIED STEAK   4 servings

1 1/2-pound beef boneless sirloin steak
Salt and pepper
1 egg, beaten
1 tablespoon water
1/2 cup soft bread crumbs (wheat bread is preferred)
1/2 cup grated Parmesan cheese
2 teaspoons dried parsley flakes
1 teaspoon minced garlic
1/2 teaspoon salt
1/2 teaspoon coarse black pepper
2 to 3 tablespoons vegetable oil
MENU: Spaghetti, spaghetti sauce, and tossed salad with salad
   dressing

1. Trim excess fat from beef. Sprinkle with salt and pepper.
2. Beat egg and water until blended. Mix bread crumbs, Parmesan cheese,
parsley, garlic, salt, and pepper. Dip beef into egg mixture. Coat with bread
crumb mixture, pressing firmly to adhere.
3. Heat oil in large skillet over medium-high heat. Place beef in skillet;
reduce heat to medium. Cook beef in oil 3 to 4 minutes. Using a spatula,
loosen breading from skillet; turn beef with spatula. Don't be concerned if
breading sticks to skillet. Pat breading back on the beef with spatula. Cook 3
to 4 minutes longer. Remove beef from skillet with spatula.

LONDON BROIL   4 servings

1 1/2-pound beef boneless sirloin steak
Pepper
3 tablespoons soy sauce
3 tablespoons Worcestershire sauce
MENU: Baked potatoes with sour cream and chives, buttered
   asparagus, and Flourless Chocolate Cake (page 176)

1. Trim excess fat from beef. Sprinkle with pepper.
2. Mix soy sauce and Worcestershire sauce in reclosable plastic bag. Place

beef in bag and close. Cover and refrigerate at least 1 hour or up to 24 hours, turning once. Drain beef, reserving marinade.

3. Heat grill. Grill beef uncovered 4 to 6 inches from medium heat 7 to 9 minutes for medium-rare or medium, turning once.

4. Heat reserved marinade to boiling; boil uncovered 1 to 2 minutes. Sauce is thin. Cut beef across grain into thin slices. Serve beef with sauce.

KANSAS CITY BROIL: Substitute 3 tablespoons steak sauce for the soy sauce. Serve with Oven-Fried Potato and Sweet Potato (page 146) and whole artichokes and butter.

CARIBBEAN FAJITAS   4 servings

1 1/2-pound beef boneless sirloin steak
Marinade:
3/4 cup pineapple juice or orange juice
1/3 cup Worcestershire sauce
1/4 cup white vinegar
1 tablespoon ground cumin
1 teaspoon garlic salt
1 teaspoon minced garlic
Flour tortillas (6 to 8 inches in diameter)
Condiments: Sour cream, salsa, and jalapeños
MENU: Rice and Black Beans (page 148) and fresh pineapple

1. Trim excess fat from beef.

2. Mix pineapple juice, Worcestershire sauce, vinegar, cumin, garlic salt, and garlic in shallow glass or plastic dish. Place beef in dish, turning to coat. Cover and refrigerate 8 to 24 hours, turning once. Drain beef, reserving marinade.

3. Heat grill. Grill beef uncovered 4 to 6 inches from medium heat 6 to 8 minutes for medium-rare to medium, turning once.

4. While beef is cooking, heat marinade to boiling. Boil 1 to 2 minutes, stirring occasionally.

5. Cut meat across grain into very thin slices. For each fajita, place a few slices of beef and desired condiments on tortilla; roll up. Serve with marinade.

STIR-FRIED FAJITAS   4 servings

1 1/2-pound beef boneless sirloin steak
Pepper
Marinade:
1/3 cup Italian salad dressing
1/3 cup soy sauce
1 large clove garlic, minced
1/2 to 1 teaspoon cornstarch, if needed
Vegetables:
1 medium green bell pepper, cut into 1/4-inch strips
1 medium red bell pepper, cut into 1/4-inch strips
1 medium onion, cut into eighths
Flour tortillas (6 to 8 inches in diameter)
Condiments: Sour cream, shredded Cheddar cheese or Monterey Jack
    cheese, guacamole, and jalapeños
MENU: Frijoles Picante (page 136) and Beef-Flavored Rice (page 151)

1. Trim excess fat from beef. Cut beef with grain into 1/2-inch strips;
sprinkle with pepper.
2. Mix all marinade ingredients except cornstarch in a reclosable plastic bag.
Stir in beef until coated. Close bag and refrigerate 1 hour. Drain meat,
reserving marinade.
3. Heat 1 tablespoon marinade in large skillet over medium-high heat. Add
beef; stir-fry about 3 minutes or until beef is light brown. Remove beef from
skillet with slotted spoon; keep warm.
4. Add peppers and onion to skillet. Stir-fry about 5 minutes or until
vegetables are crisp-tender.
5. While vegetables are cooking, heat remaining marinade to boiling in small
saucepan; boil uncovered 1 to 2 minutes. Remove saucepan from heat. If
thicker sauce is desired, sprinkle with cornstarch and stir. Stir marinade and
drained beef into vegetable mixture. Cook and stir on medium heat until
heated through and sauce is thickened.
6. For each fajita, place a few strips of beef, peppers, onion, and desired
condiments on a tortilla; roll up.

STEAK AND POTATO SALAD

Tarragon Dressing (below) or purchased dressing of your choice
Bite-size pieces romaine
Chopped green onions
Olive oil
Bite-size pieces baked potato
Bite-size pieces grilled beef sirloin steak
Green beans, cooked
Cherry tomatoes, halved
MENU: Toasted rye or pumpernickel bread

1. Prepare Tarragon Dressing.
2. Toss romaine and green onions in large serving bowl.
3. Heat oil in skillet over medium-high heat. Add potatoes; stir-fry until brown on all sides. Place potatoes on romaine.
4. Add beef to hot skillet; stir-fry 1 minute. Stir in green beans. Cook until beans are heated through, stirring occasionally. Place beef and green beans in bowl over potatoes. Top with cherry tomatoes. Serve salad with Tarragon Dressing.

TARRAGON DRESSING   about 1/3 cup

1/4 cup yogurt
2 tablespoons salad dressing or mayonnaise
2 tablespoons minced green onion
2 teaspoons lemon juice
2 teaspoons dried tarragon leaves
1/4 teaspoon salt

Mix all ingredients.

"RITZY" BAKED CHICKEN   4 servings

4 skinless boneless chicken breast halves, pounded to even thickness
Butter-flavored nonstick cooking spray
Garlic pepper
1/4 cup very finely crushed Ritz© crackers (pulverize about 7 crackers
   in food processor or blender)
1/2 teaspoon dried parsley flakes
MENU: Rice and Vermicelli (page 147) and Italian Green Bean Salad
   (page 125)

1. Heat oven to 375°. Line a 13x9x2-inch baking pan with aluminum foil and spray with nonstick cooking spray.
2. Spray chicken with nonstick cooking spray; sprinkle with garlic pepper. Mix cracker crumbs and parsley. Coat chicken with cracker crumb mixture. Place in pan. Spray with nonstick cooking spray.
3. Bake uncovered 30 to 35 minutes or until juice of chicken is longer pink when centers of thickest pieces are cut.

CAJUN OVEN-FRIED CHICKEN   4 servings

4 skinless boneless chicken breast halves, pounded to even thickness
Butter-flavored nonstick cooking spray
Salt
1 cup soft bread crumbs (wheat bread is preferred)
4 teaspoons Cajun seasoning
MENU: Cajun Pilaf (page 148) and broccoli

1. Heat oven to 375°. Line a 13x9x2-inch baking pan with aluminum foil and spray with nonstick cooking spray.
2. Spray chicken with nonstick cooking spray; sprinkle with salt. Mix bread crumbs and Cajun seasoning. Coat chicken with bread crumb mixture. Place in pan.
3. Bake uncovered 30 to 35 minutes or until juice of chicken is no longer pink when centers of thickest pieces are cut.

BAKED CHICKEN AND SAUSAGE JAMBALAYA

4 servings

1 cup rice
4 chicken breast halves with bone, skin removed
Salt and pepper
1 can (14 1/2 ounces) whole tomatoes
1 can (8 ounces) tomato sauce
1 cup chicken bouillon
1/4 cup vegetable oil
1 teaspoon Cajun seasoning
1 teaspoon dried parsley flakes
1 teaspoon minced garlic
7 ounces cooked smoked sausage links, cut into 1-inch
   pieces (about 1 1/4 cups)
1/2 cup chopped green bell pepper
MENU: Broccoli

1. Heat oven to 375°. Line a 13x9x2-inch baking pan with aluminum foil and spray with nonstick cooking spray.
2. Sprinkle rice in pan. Sprinkle chicken with salt and pepper; place chicken, breast side up, on rice.
3. Coarsely chop tomatoes, reserving juice; set tomatoes aside. Mix tomato juice, tomato sauce, and chicken bouillon. Heat to boiling in microwave or on stovetop. Stir in oil, Cajun seasoning, parsley, and garlic. Pour tomato juice mixture over chicken. Sprinkle sausage, chopped tomatoes, and green pepper into pan. Cover pan tightly with aluminum foil.
4. Bake 1 hour to 1 hour 5 minutes or until juice of chicken is no longer pink when centers of thickest pieces are cut. If excessive moisture remains, uncover and cook 5 minutes longer.

BACON-WRAPPED CHICKEN   4 servings

4 skinless boneless chicken breast halves, pounded to even thickness
Butter-flavored nonstick cooking spray
Garlic pepper
8 slices uncooked turkey bacon
1/4 cup barbecue sauce
MENU: Mashed potatoes, buttered green beans, and sliced tomatoes

1. Heat oven to 400°. Line a 13x9x2-inch baking pan with aluminum foil and spray with nonstick cooking spray.
2. Spray chicken with nonstick cooking spray and sprinkle with garlic pepper. Wrap 2 bacon slices around each chicken breast. Place in pan. Spray chicken with nonstick cooking spray.
3. Bake uncovered 25 minutes. Pour drippings from pan, if desired. Spread 1 tablespoon barbecue sauce over each chicken breast. Bake uncovered 5 to 10 minutes longer or until juice of chicken is no longer pink when centers of thickest pieces are cut.

ITALIAN BREADED CHICKEN   4 servings

4 skinless boneless chicken breast halves, pounded to even thickness
Butter-flavored nonstick cooking spray
Salt and pepper
Breading:
1/3 cup soft bread crumbs (wheat bread is preferred)
1/3 cup grated Parmesan cheese
1 teaspoon minced garlic
1/4 teaspoon dried basil leaves
1/4 teaspoon dried thyme leaves
Condiment: Spaghetti sauce
MENU: Stir-Fried Italian Vegetables (page 154) and French bread

1. Heat oven to 375°. Line a 13x9x2-inch baking pan with aluminum foil and spray with nonstick cooking spray.

2. Spray chicken with nonstick cooking spray; sprinkle with salt and pepper. Mix all breading ingredients. Coat chicken with bread crumb mixture. Place in pan.

3. Bake uncovered 30 to 35 minutes or until juice of chicken is no longer pink when centers of thickest pieces are cut.

BAKED CHICKEN WITH COLORADO SAUCE

4 servings

4 skinless boneless chicken breast halves, pounded to even thickness
Salt and pepper
4 teaspoons vegetable oil
1 teaspoon minced garlic
Colorado Sauce:
3/4 cup salsa
1 can (8 ounces) tomato sauce
1/2 cup halved black olives
1/3 cup canned whole kernel corn, drained
1/4 cup vegetable oil
1 teaspoon minced garlic
1 teaspoon dried parsley flakes
MENU: Santa Fe Rice (page 147) and zucchini

1. Heat oven to 375°. Line a 13x9x2-inch baking pan with aluminum foil and spray with nonstick cooking spray.

2. Sprinkle chicken with salt and pepper. Place in pan; drizzle with oil and sprinkle with garlic. Bake uncovered 30 to 35 minutes or until juice of chicken is no longer pink when centers of thickest pieces are cut.

3. While chicken is cooking, mix all sauce ingredients in large saucepan. Heat to boiling; reduce heat to low. Simmer uncovered 15 minutes, stirring occasionally, until sauce is thickened. Serve chicken with sauce.

SOUTHERN OVEN-FRIED CHICKEN   4 servings

4 chicken breast halves with bone, skin removed
Salt and pepper
Dried thyme leaves
Ground paprika
1/3 cup flour
1/3 cup yellow cornmeal
1/2 teaspoon salt
Butter-flavored nonstick cooking spray
MENU: Old-Fashioned Macaroni Salad (page 132) and green beans

1. Heat oven to 375°. Line a 13x9x2-inch baking pan with aluminum foil and spray with nonstick cooking spray.
2. Sprinkle chicken with salt, pepper, thyme, and paprika. Mix flour, cornmeal, and salt. Coat chicken with desired amount of flour mixture. Spray chicken with butter-flavored nonstick cooking spray. Place chicken, breast side up, in pan. For extra-crispy coating, coat top side of chicken with desired amount of additional flour mixture and spray again with nonstick cooking spray.
3. Bake uncovered 1 hour to 1 hour 5 minutes or until juice of chicken is no longer pink when centers of thickest pieces are cut.

CHINESE BAKED CHICKEN   4 servings

4 chicken breast halves with bone, skin removed
Marinade:
1 cup dry sherry
1/3 cup soy sauce
1 tablespoon ground paprika
1 1/2 teaspoons minced garlic
1/4 teaspoon coarse black pepper
MENU: Onion-Fried Rice (page 151) and sugar snap peas

1. Mix all marinade ingredients in shallow glass or plastic dish. Place chicken in marinade, turning to coat both sides. Cover and refrigerate at least 8 hours but no longer than 24 hours, turning chicken once.

2. Heat oven to 375°. Line a 13x9x2-inch baking pan with aluminum foil and spray with nonstick cooking spray.

3. Drain chicken, reserving marinade. Cover and refrigerate marinade. Place chicken, breast side up, in pan. Bake uncovered 30 minutes; baste with marinade. Discard remaining marinade. Bake uncovered 30 to 35 minutes longer or until chicken is no longer pink when centers of thickest pieces are cut. Remove chicken from oven; baste with pan drippings before serving.

TEXAS-STYLE BARBECUED CHICKEN

4 servings

4 chicken breast halves with bone, skin removed
Salt and pepper
Texas-Style Barbecue Sauce:
1/2 cup barbecue sauce (Kraft® Original Barbecue Sauce is preferred)
1/4 cup ketchup
2 tablespoons Worcestershire sauce
1 tablespoon white vinegar
1 tablespoon light brown sugar
1 teaspoon prepared mustard
1 medium clove garlic, minced

SHORTCUT:
Substitute 1 cup purchased barbecue sauce for Texas-Style Barbecue Sauce, if desired.

Garnish: 4 tablespoons canned chopped green chiles
MENU: Mexican Mashed Potatoes (page 145) and Salsa Slaw
(page 128) or purchased coleslaw

1. Heat oven to 375°. Line a 13x9x2-inch baking pan with aluminum foil and spray with nonstick cooking spray.

2. Spray chicken with nonstick cooking spray and sprinkle with salt and pepper. Place chicken, breast side up, in pan. Bake uncovered 35 minutes.

3. While chicken is cooking, mix all sauce ingredients.

4. After chicken bakes 35 minutes, pour drippings from pan. Pour sauce over chicken; sprinkle with chiles. Bake uncovered 30 to 35 minutes longer or until juice of chicken is no longer pink when centers of thickest pieces are cut.

GREEK BAKED CHICKEN   4 servings

4 skinless boneless chicken breast halves, pounded to even thickness
Garlic pepper
Dried oregano leaves
1 large clove garlic, minced
1 tablespoon olive oil
1/3 cup quartered black olives
1/2 cup crumbed feta cheese (2 ounces)
MENU: Rice or orzo and artichoke hearts drizzled with lemon juice
   and butter

1. Heat oven to 375°. Line a 13x9x2-inch baking pan with aluminum foil and
spray with nonstick cooking spray.
2. Sprinkle chicken with garlic pepper, oregano, and garlic. Place in pan.
Drizzle with olive oil.
3. Bake uncovered 30 to 35 minutes or until juice of chicken is no longer
pink when centers of thickest pieces are cut. Sprinkle black olives and feta
cheese over chicken. Bake uncovered about 5 minutes longer or until cheese
is softened.

TEX-MEX CHICKEN SANDWICHES   4 servings

4 skinless boneless chicken breast halves, pounded to even thickness
Butter-flavored nonstick cooking spray
Salt
1 cup soft bread crumbs (wheat bread is preferred)
4 teaspoons dry taco seasoning mix
8 slices bread, toasted
Salsa Mayonnaise:
1/2 cup mayonnaise or salad dressing
1/4 cup salsa
Toppings: Lettuce, sliced tomatoes, and jalapeños
MENU: Mexican Bean-Potato Salad (page 133) and tossed salad with
   salad dressing

1. Heat oven to 375°. Line a 13x9x2-inch baking pan with aluminum foil and
spray with nonstick cooking spray.

2. Spray chicken with nonstick cooking spray; sprinkle with salt. Mix bread crumbs and taco seasoning mix. Coat chicken with bread crumb mixture. Place in pan.

4. Bake uncovered 30 to 35 minutes or until juice of chicken is no longer pink when centers of thickest pieces are cut.

5. Mix mayonnaise and salsa. Spread over toast. Place chicken, lettuce, tomato, and jalapeños on each of 4 slices toast. Top with remaining toast.

FLORIDA-STYLE BARBECUED CHICKEN

4 servings

4 skinless boneless chicken breast halves, pounded to even thickness
Salt and pepper
2 teaspoons vegetable oil
Florida-Style Barbecue Sauce:
1/2 cup barbecue sauce (Kraft® Original Barbecue Sauce is preferred)
1/2 cup orange juice
1/4 cup ketchup
1/4 teaspoon coarse black pepper
2 large cloves garlic, minced
MENU: Corn-on-the-cobb and Coleslaw Pasta Salad (page 132) or
  purchased coleslaw

1. Sprinkle chicken with salt and pepper.

2. Heat oil in large skillet over medium-high heat. Cook chicken in oil 2 minutes, turning once.

3. Stir in all sauce ingredients. Heat to boiling; reduce heat to low. Cover and simmer 10 minutes. Turn chicken; cover and simmer 10 minutes longer or until juice of chicken is no longer pink when centers of thickest pieces are cut, and sauce is thickened.

FRENCH-STYLE CHICKEN 2 servings

2 skinless boneless chicken breast halves, pounded to even thickness
Salt and coarse black pepper
Flour
2 tablespoons vegetable oil
1/2 cup chicken bouillon
1/2 cup dry white wine
3 tablespoons butter
1 teaspoon dried parsley flakes
1/2 teaspoon dried thyme leaves
MENU: Rice and buttered green peas

1. Sprinkle chicken with salt and pepper. Coat with flour.
2. Heat oil in medium skillet over medium-high heat. Cook chicken in oil 5
to 7 minutes, turning once, until brown on both sides.
3. Add remaining ingredients to skillet; stir to combine. Simmer uncovered
on medium heat 10 minutes, turning once, until juice of chicken is no longer
pink when centers of thickest pieces are cut.

ROMAN-STYLE CHICKEN 4 servings

4 skinless boneless chicken breast halves, pounded to even thickness
Salt and pepper
1/4 cup butter
1 can (14 1/2 ounces) whole tomatoes
2/3 cup dry white wine
1 teaspoon minced garlic
1/2 teaspoon ground marjoram
MENU: Spaghetti, tossed salad with salad dressing, and French bread

1. Sprinkle chicken with salt and pepper.
2. Melt butter in large skillet over medium heat. Cook chicken in
butter 2 minutes, turning once.
3. Coarsely chop tomatoes, reserving juice. Add tomatoes, tomato juice,
and remaining ingredients to skillet; stir to combine. Heat to boiling;
reduce heat to medium. Cook uncovered 15 to 20 minutes, turning once,
until juice of chicken is no longer pink when centers of thickest pieces are
cut, and sauce is thickened.

POLENTA BREADED CHICKEN WITH ITALIAN GREEN BEAN SAUCE

4 servings

Italian Green Bean Sauce (below)
4 skinless boneless chicken breast halves,
  pounded to even thickness
Butter-flavored nonstick cooking spray
Salt and pepper
1/3 cup yellow cornmeal
2 1/2 tablespoons Parmesan cheese
2 teaspoons vegetable oil
MENU: Spaghetti, carrots, and Focaccia (page 44)

SHORTCUT:
Substitute 1 1/2 cups purchased spaghetti sauce for Italian Green Bean Sauce. Stir in 1 cup cooked green beans.

1. Prepare Italian Green Bean Sauce; keep warm.
2. Spray chicken with nonstick cooking spray; sprinkle with salt and pepper. Mix cornmeal and Parmesan cheese. Coat chicken with cornmeal mixture.
3. Heat oil in large skillet over medium heat. Cook chicken in oil 12 to 15 minutes, turning once, until juice of chicken is no longer pink when centers of thickest pieces are cut. Pour sauce over chicken and spaghetti.

ITALIAN GREEN BEAN SAUCE

2 1/2 cups

1 can (14 1/2 ounces) whole tomatoes, drained
1 can (8 ounces) tomato sauce
1/4 cup vegetable oil
1 teaspoon dried basil leaves
1 teaspoon dried oregano leaves
1 teaspoon dried parsley flakes
1 teaspoon sugar
1/4 teaspoon dried thyme leaves
1/4 teaspoon salt
1/4 teaspoon coarse black pepper
1 large clove garlic, minced
1 cup cooked Italian green beans or cut green beans, well drained

Coarsely chop tomatoes and drain. Mix tomatoes and remaining ingredients except green beans in large saucepan. Heat to boiling; reduce heat to low. Simmer uncovered 15 minutes. Stir in green beans and heat 3 to 5 minutes longer or until hot.

CHICKEN STROGANOFF   4 servings

1 tablespoon margarine
1 cup chopped onion
2 large cloves garlic, minced
2 tablespoons flour
1 can (10 3/4 ounces) condensed cream of chicken soup
1 can (4 ounces) sliced mushrooms, drained
1/2 teaspoon salt
1/4 teaspoon coarse black pepper
2 cups cut-up cooked chicken
3/4 to 1 cup sour cream
MENU: Egg noodles, beets, and green beans

1. Melt margarine in large skillet over medium-high heat. Cook onion and garlic in margarine, stirring frequently, until crisp-tender.
2. Stir in flour; heat until bubbly. Stir in chicken soup, mushrooms, salt, and pepper. Cook over medium heat, stirring constantly, until heated through. Stir in chicken and 3/4 cup sour cream. If thinner sauce is desired, stir in additional sour cream (up to 1/4 cup). Heat, stirring constantly, just until hot. Serve over egg noodles.

CHICKEN-MUSHROOM SAUCE: Subtitute 1 can (10 3/4 ounces) condensed cream of mushroom soup for cream of chicken soup. Serve with rice, green peas, and croissants.

CHICKEN-GREEN ONION SAUCE   4 servings

2 tablespoons butter
2 cups cut-up cooked chicken
1 teaspoon minced garlic
Salt and coarse black pepper
1 cup White Sauce (page 117 or prepared white sauce)
1 cup chopped green onions
3/4 cup grated Parmesan cheese
1/4 teaspoon coarse black pepper
Milk, if desired
MENU: Fettucine or spaghetti and buttered carrots

1. Melt butter in large skillet over medium heat. Cook chicken and garlic in butter, stirring occasionally, until hot. Sprinkle with salt and pepper.
2. Stir in remaining ingredients; cook until hot. If thinner sauce is desired, stir in milk (starting with 1 tablespoon). Serve over pasta.

CARIBBEAN CHICKEN KABOBS   2 servings

Caribbean Barbecue Sauce (below)
2 skinless boneless chicken breast halves cut into 1 1/2-inch pieces
1 medium red bell pepper, cut into 1 1/2-inch pieces
1 medium green bell pepper, cut into 1 1/2-inch pieces
1 cup fresh pineapple chunks
MENU: Rice, tossed salad with salad dressing, and Lemon Corn
**   Bread (page 36)**

1. Prepare Caribbean Barbecue Sauce.
2. Heat grill. While grill is heating, thread chicken on 3 skewers, leaving space between each piece. Thread peppers and pineapple alternately on each of 3 skewers, leaving space between each piece.
3. Cover and grill chicken and vegetables 4 to 6 inches from medium heat 10 to 15 minutes, turning once, or until juice of chicken is no longer pink in center when cut. Lightly baste chicken and vegetable kabobs with sauce during last 5 minutes of grilling. Serve chicken and vegetable kabobs with remaining sauce.

CARIBBEAN BARBECUE SAUCE   1 cup

3/4 cup chili sauce
6 tablespoons light brown sugar
2 tablespoons ketchup
2 tablespoons lime juice
1/2 teaspoon ground allspice
1/2 teaspoon ground ginger
1/2 teaspoon coarse black pepper
1/4 teaspoon salt

Mix all ingredients in small saucepan. Heat, stirring occasionally, until hot.

SOFT CHICKEN TACOS   4 servings

2 tablespoons vegetable oil, divided
1 cup chopped onion
1 teaspoon minced garlic
2 cups shredded cooked chicken
1 can (14 1/2 ounces) whole tomatoes
2 tablespoons canned chopped green chiles
2 teaspoons red wine vinegar
1 teaspoon ground cumin
1 teaspoon chili powder
1/2 teaspoon salt
1/4 teaspoon coarse black pepper
Flour tortillas (6 to 8 inches in diameter)
Condiments: Sour cream, guacamole, shredded lettuce, and shredded
  Cheddar cheese
MENU: Santa Fe Rice (page 147) and refried beans

1. Heat 1 tablespoon oil in large skillet over medium-high heat. Cook
onion and garlic in oil, stirring frequently, until crisp-tender. Stir in
remaining 1 tablespoon oil and chicken. Cook over medium heat, stirring
frequently, until chicken is brown.
2. Coarsely chop tomatoes, reserving juice. Add tomatoes, tomato juice,
green chiles, red wine vinegar, cumin, chili powder, salt, and pepper to
skillet. Heat to boiling; reduce heat to low. Simmer uncovered 10 minutes,
stirring occasionally.
3. For each taco, spoon filling and condiments on a tortilla; roll up.

CAESAR CHICKEN WRAPS   **2 servings**

2 tablespoons olive oil
1 tablespoon water
1 teaspoon garlic pepper
1 teaspoon minced garlic
1/2 teaspoon Italian seasoning
1/4 teaspoon salt
2 skinless boneless chicken breast halves, cut into 1/2-inch strips
1 tablespoon olive oil (for skillet)
Flour tortillas (6 to 8 inches in diameter)
Condiment: Creamy Caesar Salad Dressing (page 120) or purchased
   Caesar salad dressing
MENU: Basil Oven-Fried Potatoes (page 143) and Tomato-Green
   Pepper Salad (page 135)

1. Mix 2 tablespoons olive oil, water, garlic pepper, garlic, Italian seasoning, and salt in a shallow glass or plastic dish. Stir in chicken strips until coated. Cover and refrigerate at least 30 minutes or up to 24 hours.
2. Heat 1 tablespoon olive oil in large skillet over medium-high heat. Stir in chicken and marinade. Stir-fry 5 to 7 minutes or until chicken is no longer pink when cut.
3. For each wrap, place a few strips of chicken on a tortilla. Drizzle with Creamy Caesar Salad Dressing; roll up.

CAESAR CHICKEN SALAD: Omit flour tortillas and suggested menu. Arrange cooked chicken strips on top of mixed salad greens; sprinkle with croutons and shredded Parmesan cheese. Serve with Creamy Caesar Salad Dressing (page 120) or purchased Caesar salad dressing.

TEX-MEX CHICKEN MANICOTTI   4 servings

1/2 cup Enchilada Sauce (page 118 or purchased enchilada
    sauce), divided
1 cup cut-up cooked chicken
3/4 cup low-fat cottage cheese, drained
1/3 cup cubed Monterey Jack cheese
1/4 cup chopped green onions
1/4 cup grated Parmesan cheese
1 egg
1 medium clove garlic, minced
1/2 teaspoon salt
1/4 teaspoon coarse black pepper
8 cooked manicotti shells
Garnish: 1 cup shredded Monterey Jack cheese (4 ounces) and chopped
    green onions
MENU: Rice and Black Beans (page 148), tossed salad with salad
    dressing, and French bread

1. Heat oven to 375°. Line an 11x7x2-inch baking dish with aluminum
foil and spray with nonstick cooking spray. Spread about 1/4 cup
enchilada sauce in bottom of baking dish.
2. Mix chicken, cottage cheese, cubed Monterey Jack cheese, green onions,
Parmesan cheese, egg, garlic, salt, and pepper. Fill the cooked manicotti
shells with the chicken mixture. Place shells on sauce. Pour remaining
1/4 cup sauce over shells, covering shells completely.
3. Cover and bake 25 minutes. Sprinkle with shredded Monterey Jack
cheese. Bake uncovered 5 minutes longer or until cheese is melted. Garnish
with green onion. Let stand 5 minutes before serving.

CHICKEN AND CHEESE CHIMICHANGAS

8 chimichangas

1 teaspoon vegetable oil
1/2 cup minced onion
1 large clove garlic, minced
2 cups cut-up cooked chicken
1 1/4 cups shredded Cheddar or Monterey Jack cheese (5 ounces)
1/4 teaspoon salt
1/4 teaspoon coarse black pepper
2 cans (8 ounces each) refrigerated crescent rolls
Condiments: Sour cream, salsa, and guacamole
MENU: Santa Fe Rice (page 147), refried beans, and tossed
  salad with salad dressing

1. Heat oven to 350°. Line a baking sheet with aluminum foil and grease
with shortening.
2. Heat oil in large skillet over medium-high heat. Cook onion and garlic in
oil, stirring frequently, until onion is crisp-tender. Remove pan from heat;
stir in chicken, cheese, salt, and pepper.
3. Separate dough into 8 rectangles. Firmly press perforations to seal. Divide
chicken filling evenly among the rectangles, mounding the filling at one end.
Fold end over filling. Fold sides of rectangle inward. Starting at folded end,
roll up. Place seam side down on baking sheet.
4. Bake uncovered 20 to 25 minutes or until golden brown. Serve with
condiments.

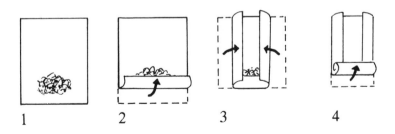

1   2   3   4

CHINESE CHICKEN SALAD   2 servings

Oriental Dressing (below)
2 cups cut-up cooked chicken
4 cups bite-size pieces spinach
4 slices bacon, crisply cooked and crumbled
1 cup broccoli florets (4 ounces)
1 can (8 ounces) sliced water chestnuts, drained
1/2 cup chopped green onions
3 radishes, sliced
Garnish: Shredded Parmesan cheese
MENU: Hard rolls

1. Prepare Oriental Dressing.
2. Mix chicken, spinach, bacon, broccoli, water chestnuts, green onions, and radishes in large glass or plastic bowl. Serve salad with shredded Parmesan cheese and Oriental Dressing.

ORIENTAL DRESSING   about 3/4 cup

1/2 cup vegetable oil
3 tablespoons soy sauce
2 tablespoons honey
2 tablespoons sugar
1 tablespoon ketchup
1/2 teaspoon dried minced onion
1/8 teaspoon coarse black pepper

Shake all ingredients in tightly covered container.

FIESTA CHICKEN SALAD   4 servings

Cheese Salad Dressing (below)
4 skinless boneless chicken breast halves, cut into 1/2-inch strips
1 teaspoon chili powder
1 teaspoon ground cumin
1/2 teaspoon salt
1 tablespoon vegetable oil
Salad:
8 cups bite-size pieces romaine
1 can (15 ounces) black beans, rinsed and drained
1 cup chopped green onions
4 radishes, sliced
Garnish: 10 to 12 cherry tomatoes, halved, and tortilla chips
MENU: Herb Corn Bread (page 36)

1. Prepare Cheese Salad Dressing; keep warm.
2. Place chicken strips in large bowl; toss with chili powder, cumin, and salt.
3. Heat oil in large skillet over medium-high heat. Cook chicken in oil 5 to 7 minutes, stirring frequently, until chicken is no longer pink in center when cut. Drain chicken.
4. Mix romaine, black beans, green onions, and radishes in large bowl. Arrange chicken strips on top of romaine mixture, radiating from center of the bowl like the spokes of a wheel. Place tomato halves in center of bowl. Line rim of bowl with tortilla chips. Pass Cheese Salad Dressing.
NOTE: Serve salad in 4 individual bowls, if preferred.

CHEESE SALAD DRESSING   about 2 3/4 cups

1 pound process cheese spread loaf, cut into pieces (Velveeta® is
   preferred)
3/4 cup salsa
Milk, if desired

Place process cheese and salsa in large microwavable bowl. Heat in microwave on High (100%), stopping and stirring, until cheese is melted. If thinner sauce is desired, stir in milk (starting with 1 tablespoon). Serve immediately or cover and refrigerate until ready to serve. Reheat before serving.

CAJUN HEN   4 servings

3 1/2- to 4-pound broiler-fryer chicken, giblets removed
Salt
Cajun seasoning
MENU: Rice and Red Beans (page 149) and fried okra

1. Heat oven to 375°. Line a shallow baking pan with aluminum foil and spray with nonstick cooking spray.
2. Trim excess fat from chicken. Cut chicken lengthwise along backbone from tail to neck with sharp knife or kitchen scissors. Split open to lay flat, cracking the bone. Place chicken, skin side up, in pan. Sprinkle with salt; rub Cajun seasoning into chicken skin.
3. Roast uncovered 1 1/4 to 1 1/2 hours or until instant-read thermometer reads 180° and juice of chicken is no longer pink when center of thigh is cut. Let stand 15 minutes for easiest carving.

SIMON AND GARFUNKEL CORNISH HEN   2 to 4 servings

2 Rock Cornish hens (20 ounces each), giblets removed
Salt and coarse black pepper
Dried parsley flakes
Rubbed sage
Dried rosemary leaves
Dried thyme leaves
MENU: Mushroom Risotto (page 149) and Two-Bean Salad (page 125)

1. Heat oven to 400°. Line a shallow baking pan with aluminum foil and spray with nonstick cooking spray.
2. Trim excess fat from hens. Rinse cavity of hens. Lightly salt cavity. Rub salt, pepper, parsley, sage, rosemary, and thyme into hen skin. Place hens, breast side up, in pan.
3. Roast uncovered 30 minutes. Reduce heat to 375° and roast uncovered 30 minutes longer or until instant-read thermometer reads 180° and juice of hen is no longer pink when center of thigh is cut.

PEKING DUCK　　　4 servings

4 1/2- to 5-pound duckling, giblets removed
Salt and coarse black pepper
1/2 cup barbecue sauce (Kraft® Original Barbecue Sauce is preferred)
1/4 cup strawberry preserves
2 tablespoons honey
1 tablespoon soy sauce
Flour tortillas (6 to 8 inches in diameter)
Chopped green onions
MENU: Pepper-Fried Rice (page 151) and Mandarin Snow
** Peas (page 152)**

1. Heat oven to 350°. Line a shallow baking pan with aluminum foil.
2. Trim excess fat from duckling. Rinse and drain. Score skin with sharp knife at 1-inch intervals for crisp skin. Sprinkle cavity of duckling with salt and pepper. Place duckling, breast side up, in pan. Sprinkle with salt and pepper.
3. Mix barbecue sauce, strawberry preserves, honey, and soy sauce. Brush duckling with some of the sauce. Cover and refrigerate remaining sauce. Roast uncovered 1 hour. Pour drippings from pan. (CAUTION: A large accumulation of fat can cause an oven fire.) Place tent of aluminum foil loosely over breast to prevent excessive browning. Reduce heat to 325°. Roast duckling 1 hour and 30 minutes longer or until instant-read thermometer reads 180° and juice is no longer pink when center of thigh is cut. Let stand 15 minutes for easiest carving. While duckling rests, heat sauce.
4. Spread tortilla with some sauce, top with slices of duckling, and sprinkle with green onions; fold tortilla in half. Serve with remaining sauce.

TEX-MEX QUICHE   4 servings

2 cups shredded Monterey Jack cheese with jalapeños (8 ounces)
1 jar (2 ounces) chopped pimientos, well drained (1/4 cup)
1/4 cup chopped green onions
1 cup baking mix
1 cup milk
4 eggs
1/2 teaspoon salt
MENU: Panfried potatoes, sliced peaches, and buttered toast

1. Heat oven to 375°. Spray a 9-inch pie plate with nonstick cooking spray.
Sprinkle cheese into pie plate; sprinkle pimientos and green onions over
cheese.
2. Place baking mix, milk, eggs, and salt in blender. Cover and blend on high
speed for 15 seconds. Pour egg mixture over cheese mixture. Do not stir.
3. Bake uncovered 25 to 30 minutes or until light golden brown. Let stand 5
minutes before serving.

GREEN ONION OMELET   1 to 2 servings

3 eggs
1 tablespoon water
1/2 cup chopped green onions
1/8 teaspoon salt
1/8 teaspoon coarse black pepper
3 to 4 slices process American cheese
Garnish: Chopped green onions
MENU: Oven-Fried Potatoes (page 143) and strawberries

1. Beat eggs and water with fork until blended. Stir in green onions, salt, and
pepper.
2. Spray a medium skillet with nonstick cooking spray; heat over medium-
high heat. Pour egg mixture into skillet. Use fork to spread eggs
continuously over bottom of skillet as they thicken. Let stand over heat to
lightly brown bottom of omelet.
3. Top omelet with cheese. Broil until cheese is melted. Tilt skillet and slip
spatula under omelet to loosen eggs from bottom of skillet. Fold omelet in
half; slide omelet onto serving platter. Sprinkle with chopped green onions.

ITALIAN POACHED EGGS   2 servings

4 eggs
Salt and pepper
1 cup warm spaghetti sauce
4 ounces sliced mozzarella cheese
2 tablespoons grated Parmesan cheese
MENU: Polenta (page 142) or prepared polenta, sliced cantaloupe, and
    Italian Beer Muffins (page 24)

1. Spray a medium skillet with nonstick cooking spray; heat over medium heat. Carefully slip each egg into skillet. Sprinkle with salt and pepper. Immediately reduce heat to low. Cook 5 minutes or until whites are set; turn eggs.
2. Gently pour warm spaghetti sauce into skillet. Cook over low heat until eggs are cooked to desired doneness.
3. Top with sliced mozzarella cheese and sprinkle with Parmesan cheese. Broil briefly to melt cheeses.

MEXICAN POACHED EGGS: Substitute 1 cup warm salsa or picante sauce for the spaghetti sauce and 4 ounces sliced Monterey Jack or Cheddar cheese for mozzarella cheese. Omit Parmesan cheese, if desired. Serve with rice or refried beans and Pineapple-Coconut Muffins (page 23).

PARMESAN FISH   2 servings

2/3 pound orange roughy fillets, about 1/2 inch thick
Butter-flavored nonstick cooking spray
Salt and pepper
1/3 cup soft bread crumbs (wheat bread is preferred)
1/3 cup grated Parmesan cheese
MENU: Spaghetti, spaghetti sauce, and buttered green beans

1. Heat oven to 350°. Line an 11x7x2-inch baking dish with aluminum foil and spray with nonstick cooking spray.
2. Cut fish fillets into serving pieces. Spray fish with butter-flavored nonstick cooking spray. Sprinkle both sides of fish with salt and pepper. Mix bread crumbs and Parmesan cheese. Coat fish with bread crumb mixture, pressing to adhere. Place in dish.
3. Bake uncovered 25 to 30 minutes or until fish flakes easily with fork.

GREEK-STYLE BAKED FISH   2 servings

1/2 pound orange roughy fillets, about 1/2 inch thick
Garlic pepper
Dried oregano leaves
1 tablespoon olive oil
1/4 cup chopped black olives
1/3 cup coarsely crumbled feta cheese (about 1 1/2 ounces)
MENU: Rice or orzo and whole artichokes with melted butter

1. Heat oven to 350°. Line an 11x7x2-inch baking dish with aluminum foil
and spray with nonstick cooking spray.
2. Cut fish fillets into serving pieces. Sprinkle both sides of fish with garlic
pepper and oregano. Place in dish. Drizzle olive oil over fish.
3. Bake uncovered 25 minutes. Sprinkle black olives and feta cheese over
fish. Bake uncovered 3 to 5 minutes longer or until fish flakes easily with
fork and cheese is softened.

CHILI-ONION BAKED FISH   2 servings

2/3 pound halibut fillets, about 1/2 inch thick
Butter-flavored nonstick cooking spray
Salt and pepper
1/3 cup chili sauce
3 tablespoons minced onion
1 slice process American cheese, cut into 1/2-inch strips
MENU: Garlic Mashed Potatoes (page 145) and green peas

1. Heat oven to 350°. Line an 11x7x2-inch baking dish with aluminum foil
and spray with nonstick cooking spray.
2. Cut fish fillets into serving pieces. Spray with butter-flavored nonstick
cooking spray. Sprinkle both sides of fish with salt and pepper. Place in dish.
3. Bake uncovered 15 minutes. Pour drippings from dish, if desired. Mix
chili sauce and onion. Spread desired amount of chili sauce mixture over
fish; bake uncovered 10 minutes longer. Arrange cheese strips over fish;
bake uncovered 3 to 5 minutes longer or until cheese melts. Heat remaining
chili sauce mixture and serve with fish.

CORNFLAKE-CRUSTED FISH   4 servings

1 pound red snapper fillets, about 1/2 inch thick
Salt and pepper
1 egg white
2 cups crushed cornflakes cereal
Condiments: Lemon wedges and Creamy Cocktail Sauce (below) or
  purchased cocktail sauce
MENU: Panfried yellow squash and tossed salad with salad dressing

1. Heat oven to 350°. Line a 13x9x2-inch baking pan with aluminum foil and spray with nonstick cooking spray.
2. Cut fish fillets into serving pieces. Sprinkle both sides of fish with salt and pepper. Beat egg white until frothy. Dip fish into egg white; coat with desired amount of cornflakes, pressing to adhere. Place in pan.
3. Bake uncovered 25 to 30 minutes or until fish flakes easily with fork. Serve fish with lemon wedges and Creamy Cocktail Sauce.

CREAMY COCKTAIL SAUCE   3/4 cup

1/2 cup ketchup
1/4 cup sour cream
2 teaspoons prepared horseradish

Mix all ingredients in small glass or plastic bowl. Serve with fish or shrimp.

COCKTAIL SAUCE   1/2 cup

1/2 cup ketchup or chili sauce
2 teaspoons prepared horseradish
1 teaspoon lemon juice

Mix all ingredients in small glass or plastic bowl. Serve with fish or shrimp.

HERB-CRUSTED FISH   2 servings

2/3 to 3/4 pound salmon fish fillets, about 1/2 inch thick
Butter-flavored nonstick cooking spray
Salt and coarse black pepper
Topping:
1/2 cup soft bread crumbs (wheat bread is preferred)
1/2 teaspoon dried parsley flakes
1/2 teaspoon dried dill weed
1/4 teaspoon dried basil leaves
1/8 teaspoon pepper
Condiment: Herb Tartar Sauce (below)
MENU: Mashed potatoes and carrots with green peas

1. Heat oven to 350°. Line an 11x7x2-inch baking dish with aluminum foil
and spray with nonstick cooking spray.
2. Cut fish fillets into serving pieces. Spray with butter-flavored nonstick
cooking spray. Sprinkle both sides of fish with salt and pepper. Place in dish.
3. Mix all topping ingredients. Sprinkle topping over fish; press to adhere.
Sprinkle with salt.
4. Bake uncovered 22 to 25 minutes or until fish flakes easily with fork.

HERB TARTAR SAUCE   1/3 cup

1/4 cup salad dressing
1 tablespoon chopped Kosher dill pickle
1 tablespoon minced onion
1 1/2 teaspoons Kosher dill pickle juice
1 teaspoon dried dill weed
1 teaspoon dried chives

Mix all ingredients in small glass or plastic bowl. Serve with fish or shrimp.

BAKED CAJUN PO' BOYS   2 servings

1/2 pound catfish fillets, about 1/2 inch thick
Butter-flavored nonstick cooking spray
1/2 cup soft bread crumbs (wheat bread is preferred)
2 teaspoons Cajun seasoning
Hamburger buns
Condiments: Green Olive Tartar Sauce (below) or purchased
  tartar sauce, and shredded lettuce
MENU: Corn-Tomato Salad (page 129) and potato chips

1. Heat oven to 350°. Line an 11x7x2-inch baking dish with aluminum foil
and spray with nonstick cooking spray.
2. Cut fish fillets into 2x1 1/2-inch pieces. Spray fish with butter-flavored
nonstick cooking spray. Mix bread crumbs and Cajun seasoning; coat fish
with bread crumb mixture, pressing to adhere. Place in dish.
3. Bake uncovered 25 to 30 minutes or until fish flakes easily with fork.
Serve fish on buns.

GREEN OLIVE TARTAR SAUCE   1/3 cup

1/4 cup salad dressing
1 tablespoon chopped Kosher dill pickle
1 tablespoon chopped pimiento-stuffed green olives
1 tablespoon minced onion
1 1/2 teaspoons Kosher dill pickle juice

Mix all ingredients in small glass or plastic bowl. Serve with fish or shrimp.

BASIL TARTAR SAUCE   1/3 cup

1/4 cup salad dressing
2 tablespoons chopped fresh basil leaves
1 tablespoon chopped Kosher dill pickle
1 tablespoon minced onion
1 1/2 teaspoons Kosher dill pickle juice

Mix all ingredients in small glass or plastic bowl. Cover and
refrigerate 30 minutes before serving. Serve with fish or shrimp.

CAJUN FRIED FISH   2 servings

1/2 pound catfish fillets, about 1/2 inch thick
Cajun seasoning
Flour
2 teaspoons vegetable oil
Condiments: Ketchup or chili sauce
MENU: French fries, Colorful Coleslaw (page 128) or purchased
  coleslaw, and sliced tomatoes

1. Cut fish fillets into serving pieces. Sprinkle both sides of fish with Cajun seasoning; coat with flour.
2. Heat oil in medium skillet over medium heat. Fry fish in oil 6 to 10 minutes, turning fish once, until fish flakes easily with fork.

TARTAR SAUCE   2/3 cup

1/2 cup salad dressing or mayonnaise
2 tablespoons chopped Kosher dill pickle
2 tablespoons minced onion
1 tablespoon Kosher dill pickle juice

Mix all ingredients in small glass or plastic bowl. Serve with fish or shrimp.

GARLIC FISH   2 servings

1/2 pound mahi-mahi fillets, about 1/2 inch thick
Salt and pepper
1 tablespoon vegetable oil
2 teaspoons minced garlic
MENU: Chicken-Flavored Rice (page 151) and zucchini

1. Cut fish fillets into serving pieces. Sprinkle both sides of fish with salt and pepper.
2. Heat oil in medium skillet over medium heat. Fry fish in oil 6 to 8 minutes, turning fish once. Sprinkle garlic into skillet; fry 1 to 2 minutes or until fish flakes easily with fork.

MEXICAN FRIED FISH WITH VERACRUZ SAUCE

4 servings

Veracruz Sauce (below)
1 pound orange roughy fillets, about 1/2 inch thick
Salt and coarse black pepper
Dry taco seasoning mix
Flour
2 tablespoons vegetable oil
MENU: Rice, Mexican-Style Tossed Salad (page 124) with salad
   dressing, flour tortillas, and Lime Cream Pie (page 169)

1. Prepare Veracruz Sauce; keep warm.
2. Cut fish fillets into serving pieces. Sprinkle both sides of fish with salt and pepper. Rub surface of fish with taco seasoning mix; coat with flour.
3. Heat oil in large skillet over medium heat. Place fish in skillet; reduce heat to low. Fry fish in oil 6 to 10 minutes, turning fish once, until fish flakes easily with fork. Serve fish with Veracruz Sauce.

VERACRUZ SAUCE

about 1 1/2 cups

1 1/4 cups salsa
1/3 cup halved pimiento-stuffed green olives
2 teaspoons capers, drained

Mix salsa, green olives, and capers in small saucepan. Heat until hot.

MEXICAN COCKTAIL SAUCE

1/2 cup

1/2 cup salsa
1 teaspoon prepared horseradish

Mix all ingredients in small glass or plastic bowl. Serve with fish or shrimp.

BAJA SAUCE

2/3 cup

1/3 cup salad dressing or mayonnaise
1/3 cup yogurt

Mix all ingredients in small glass or plastic bowl. Serve with fish or shrimp.

TUNA-SALSA POTATO TOPPER   2 servings

2 large baking potatoes
1 can (6 ounces) solid albacore tuna in water, drained
2/3 cup salsa
1/3 cup chopped black olives
1/8 teaspoon salt
1/8 teaspoon coarse black pepper
Condiment: Easy Cheesy Sauce (page 117) or shredded Cheddar
  cheese
MENU: Peas and carrots

1. Cook potatoes in oven or microwave until tender. Set aside.
2. Mix tuna, salsa, black olives, salt, and pepper in microwavable bowl;
cover loosely with plastic wrap. Heat in microwave on High (100%) 1 to 2
minutes, stopping and stirring, until hot.
3. Split open each potato; spoon tuna mixture into potato. Drizzle with Easy
Cheesy Sauce or sprinkle with shredded cheese.

SPAGHETTI AND   2 servings
TUNA-TOMATO SAUCE

1 can (14 1/2 ounces) whole tomatoes, drained
1 can (8 ounces) tomato sauce
1/2 cup chopped onion
2 tablespoons olive oil
1 teaspoon minced garlic
1 teaspoon dried parsley flakes
1 teaspoon dried basil leaves
1/4 teaspoon salt
1/4 teaspoon coarse black pepper
1 can (6 ounces) chunk albacore tuna in water, drained
MENU: Spaghetti, tossed salad with salad dressing, and French bread

1. Coarsely chop tomatoes and drain. Mix tomatoes and remaining
ingredients except tuna in large saucepan.
2. Heat to boiling; reduce heat to low. Simmer uncovered 15 minutes,
stirring occasionally. Stir in tuna. Cook about 2 minutes, stirring
occasionally, until hot. Serve sauce over spaghetti.

CLAM CARBONARA   2 servings

1 can (6 1/2 ounces) chopped clams
4 eggs
6 tablespoons grated Parmesan cheese
1 teaspoon dried parsley flakes
1/4 teaspoon salt
1/4 teaspoon coarse black pepper
2 tablespoons margarine
2 large cloves garlic, minced
2 cups hot cooked spaghetti
MENU: Italian-Style Tossed Salad (page 123) with salad dressing and
   breadsticks

1. Drain clams, reserving 2 tablespoons liquid. Mix clams, 2 tablespoons
reserved liquid, eggs, Parmesan cheese, parsley, salt, and pepper in large
bowl.
2. Melt margarine in large skillet over medium heat. Cook garlic in
margarine 1 minute. Stir in egg mixture and cooked spaghetti. Cook until
mixture is thickened throughout but still moist, stirring occasionally.

QUICK-AND-EASY CRAB CAKES   4 crab cakes

1 can (6 1/2 ounces) white crabmeat, drained
1 egg
1 slice bread, torn into pieces (wheat bread is preferred)
1 tablespoon salad dressing or mayonnaise
2 teaspoons Dijon mustard
1/4 teaspoon salt
1/4 teaspoon coarse black pepper
Condiment: Ketchup
MENU: Onion-Flavored Oven-Fried Potatoes (page 143) and
   broccoli

1. Mix all ingredients. Shape mixture into 4 patties.
2. Spray a medium skillet with nonstick cooking spray; heat over medium
heat. Fry patties 4 to 5 minutes, turning once, until golden brown on both
sides.

SHRIMP TACOS   2 servings

2/3 pound uncooked medium shrimp, peeled and deveined
3 to 4 teaspoons dry taco seasoning mix
Pepper
Flour tortillas (6 to 8 inches in diameter)
Condiments: Salsa, sour cream, and shredded Monterey Jack
  cheese
MENU: Rice and tossed salad with Parmesan Salad Dressing
  (page 121)

1. Heat oven to 350°. Line a shallow baking pan with aluminum foil and spray with nonstick cooking spray.
2. Rinse shrimp and drain. Dry thoroughly, blotting with paper towel to remove moisture. Place shrimp on ceramic or plastic plate. Coat shrimp with taco seasoning mix; sprinkle with pepper. Place shrimp in pan; spray with nonstick cooking spray.
3. Bake uncovered 20 to 25 minutes or until shrimp are pink and firm.
4. For each taco, place shrimp on tortilla. Top with desired condiments; roll up.

CAJUN SHRIMP WRAPS: Omit taco seasoning mix, suggested condiments, and menu. Spray shrimp with butter-flavored nonstick cooking spray; coat shrimp with 2 teaspoons Cajun seasoning. Bake as directed for Shrimp Tacos. For each wrap, spread flour tortilla with butter, then top with shrimp. Serve with French fries, coleslaw, and Creamy Cocktail Sauce (page 81).

BACON-WRAPPED SHRIMP   2 servings

1/2 pound uncooked large shrimp, peeled and deveined
1/2 pound sliced bacon, each slice cut into thirds or fourths
1/4 cup barbecue sauce (Kraft® Original Barbecue Sauce is preferred)
1/4 cup orange juice
2 tablespoons ketchup
1 large clove garlic, minced
1/8 teaspoon coarse black pepper
MENU: Rice and Tomato-Green Pepper Salad (page 135) served
  on salad greens

1. Heat oven to 350°. Line a shallow baking pan with aluminum foil.
2. Wrap each shrimp with bacon slice; secure with toothpick, if desired. Place in pan.
3. Bake uncovered 25 to 30 minutes or until bacon is crisp, and shrimp are pink and firm.
4. While shrimp are baking, mix barbecue sauce, orange juice, ketchup, garlic, and pepper in small saucepan. Heat to boiling; reduce to simmer. Simmer uncovered 5 minutes. Serve shrimp with sauce.

CREOLE SAUCE about 3 1/4 cups

1/4 cup butter
3/4 cup chopped onion
3/4 cup chopped celery
3/4 cup chopped green bell pepper
1 can (14 1/2 ounces) whole tomatoes
1 can (8 ounces) tomato sauce
1 1/2 teaspoons minced garlic
1 teaspoon sugar
2 bay leaves
3/4 teaspoon dried oregano leaves
1/2 teaspoon chicken bouillon granules
1/2 teaspoon dried basil leaves
1/2 teaspoon dried thyme leaves
1/2 teaspoon paprika
1/2 teaspoon salt
1/2 teaspoon coarse black pepper
MENU: Boiled shrimp or panfried steak, rice, and green beans

Don't be intimidated by the long list of ingredients. This recipe is very easy to prepare.

1. Melt butter in large saucepan over medium heat. Cook onion, celery, and green pepper in butter about 5 minutes, stirring occasionally, until vegetables are crisp-tender.
2. Coarsely chop tomatoes, reserving juice. Stir in tomatoes, tomato juice, and remaining ingredients. Heat to boiling; reduce heat to low. Simmer uncovered 20 minutes, stirring occasionally. Remove bay leaves. Serve sauce over boiled shrimp or panfried steak.

SHRIMP PICANTE   2 servings

Picante Sauce (below)
2/3 pound uncooked medium shrimp, peeled and deveined
Salt
MENU: Spaghetti, tossed salad with Pesto Salad Dressing (page 121), and Coiled Bread (page 45)

1. Prepare Picante Sauce; keep warm.
2. Heat about 2 cups water to boiling in saucepan. Add shrimp. Heat to boiling; reduce heat to low. Cover and simmer 3 to 5 minutes or until shrimp are pink and firm; drain. Sprinkle lightly with salt.
3. Place spaghetti on individual serving plates. Top with shrimp; pour over desired amount of Picante Sauce.

PICANTE SAUCE   2 1/2 to 3 cups

1 can (14 1/2 ounces) Mexican-style stewed tomatoes
1 can (8 ounces) tomato sauce
1/3 cup chopped green onions
1/3 cup minced onion
2 to 3 tablespoons ketchup
2 tablespoons red wine vinegar
1 tablespoon canned chopped green chile
1 large clove garlic, minced

Mix all ingredients in large saucepan. Heat to boiling; reduce heat to low. Simmer uncovered 10 minutes, stirring occasionally. Serve hot or cold.

ITALIAN BREADED SHRIMP   2 servings

1/2 to 2/3 pound uncooked medium-to-large shrimp, peeled and deveined
Salt and pepper
3 tablespoons Italian bread crumbs
3 tablespoons grated Parmesan cheese
1 tablespoon vegetable oil
MENU: Spaghetti, spaghetti sauce, and broccoli

1. Rinse shrimp and drain. Dry thoroughly, blotting with paper towel to remove moisture.

2. Spray shrimp with nonstick cooking spray; sprinkle with salt and pepper. Mix bread crumbs and Parmesan cheese. Coat shrimp with bread crumb mixture; reserve leftover bread crumb mixture.

3. Heat oil in medium skillet over medium heat. Add shrimp to skillet; reduce heat to low. Fry shrimp in oil 3 to 4 minutes. Sprinkle with preferred amount of the reserved bread crumbs if thicker crust is desired; spray with nonstick cooking spray. Turn; fry 3 to 4 minutes longer or until crust is brown and shrimp are firm.

LOW COUNTRY SHRIMP BOIL   2 servings

8 cups chicken bouillon
2 to 3 teaspoons Chesapeake Bay style seafood seasoning
2 large cloves garlic, peeled
2 medium unpeeled potatoes, cut into fourths
5 ounces smoked sausage links, cut into 2-inch slices (1 cup, heaping)
4 frozen half-ears corn-on-the-cob
1/2 to 2/3 pound uncooked large shrimp in shells
Salt
Butter
Condiments: Creamy Cocktail Sauce (page 81) or purchased cocktail
  sauce
MENU: Sliced cucumbers with salad dressing, French bread, and
  Lemon Cream Pie (page 169)

1. Heat chicken bouillon, seafood seasoning, and garlic to boiling in a stockpot. Stir in potatoes and sausage; heat to boiling. Cover and boil 8 minutes.

2. Add corn. Heat to boiling; cover and boil 3 to 5 minutes or until potatoes are almost done.

3. Stir in shrimp. Heat to boiling; cover and boil 5 to 7 minutes or until shrimp are pink and firm; drain. (Reserve cooking liquid if you want to use it as a dip for bread.)

4. Arrange shrimp and vegetables on large platter. Sprinkle with salt and drizzle with butter, if desired.

GREEK-STYLE SHRIMP   2 servings

1/2 to 2/3 pound uncooked medium shrimp, peeled and deveined
Greek Tomato Sauce:
1 can (14 1/2 ounces) whole tomatoes
1/4 cup olive oil
2 tablespoons tomato paste
1 tablespoon balsamic vinegar, scant
1 teaspoon minced garlic
1 teaspoon dried oregano leaves
1 teaspoon dried basil leaves
1 teaspoon dried parsley flakes
1 teaspoon sugar
1/4 teaspoon salt
1/4 teaspoon coarse black pepper
1 cup cubed feta cheese (4 ounces)
MENU: Rice or orzo and spinach salad with salad dressing

1. Coarsely chop tomatoes, reserving juice. Mix tomatoes, tomato juice, and remaining ingredients except shrimp and feta cheese in large saucepan. Heat to boiling; reduce heat to low. Simmer uncovered, stirring occasionally, 12 to 15 minutes or until sauce is thickened; keep warm.
2. While sauce is cooking prepare shrimp. Heat about 2 cups water to boiling in saucepan. Add shrimp. Heat to boiling; reduce heat to low. Cover and simmer 3 to 5 minutes or until shrimp are pink and firm; drain. Sprinkle lightly with salt.
3. Add shrimp and feta cheese to warm sauce; gently stir to combine. Serve sauce over rice.

GARLIC SHRIMP   2 servings

1/2 to 2/3 pound uncooked medium shrimp, peeled and deveined
1 tablespoon butter
1 teaspoon minced garlic
1/8 teaspoon dried basil leaves
1/8 teaspoon dried oregano leaves
1/8 teaspoon salt
1/8 teaspoon coarse black pepper
MENU: Herbed Spaghetti (page 140) or spaghetti, tossed salad with
    salad dressing, and Parmesan Corn Bread (page 36)

1. Rinse shrimp and drain. Dry thoroughly, blotting with paper towel to remove moisture.

2. Melt butter in medium skillet over medium heat. Cook shrimp in butter 4 to 8 minutes, turning once. Stir in garlic; cook 1 minute. Sprinkle shrimp with basil, oregano, salt, and pepper. Toss to coat. Scrap skillet with spatula to loosen browned bits, if desired. Serve shrimp over spaghetti.

CHILI-BEAN HOT DOGS   4 hot dogs

4 hot dogs
4 hot dog buns
Chili-Bean Sauce:
1 can (14 1/2 ounces) whole tomatoes, drained
1 can (15 ounces) red kidney beans, rinsed and drained
1 can (8 ounces) tomato sauce
1/4 cup vegetable oil
1 to 2 tablespoons canned chopped green chiles
1 1/4 teaspoons chili powder
1 teaspoon ground cumin
1 teaspoon minced garlic
1/4 teaspoon salt
1/4 teaspoon coarse black pepper
Condiments: Ketchup, mustard, hot dog relish, chopped onion,
  and shredded Cheddar cheese
MENU: Chili-Flavored Oven-Fried Potatoes (page 143) and tossed salad
  with salad dressing

1. Heat grill and cook hot dogs.

2. While hot dogs are cooking, prepare sauce. Coarsely chop tomatoes and drain. Mix tomatoes and remaining sauce ingredients in large saucepan. Heat to boiling; reduce heat to low. Simmer uncovered 10 to 15 minutes, stirring occasionally, until sauce is thickened. Place hot dogs in buns. Top with Chili-Bean Sauce and condiments.

ITALIAN HAMBURGERS   4 hamburgers

1 pound lean ground beef
2 tablespoons grated Parmesan cheese
1 tablespoon tomato paste
1 teaspoon dried parsley flakes
3/4 teaspoon salt
1/2 teaspoon dried basil leaves
1/2 teaspoon dried oregano leaves
1/4 teaspoon coarse black pepper
1 teaspoon minced garlic
4 hamburger buns
Condiments: Sliced mozzarella cheese and pizza sauce or ketchup
MENU: Basil Oven-Fried Potatoes (page 143) and Italian-Style Tossed
   Salad (page 123) with salad dressing

1. Mix all ingredients except hamburger buns. Shape mixture into 4 patties.
2. Heat grill. Grill patties uncovered about 4 inches from medium heat 14
to 18 minutes, turning once, until no longer pink in center and juice is clear.
Serve on buns.

CAJUN HAMBURGERS   4 hamburgers

1 pound lean ground beef
2 tablespoons ketchup
4 teaspoons Cajun seasoning
3/4 teaspoon salt
4 hamburger buns
Condiments: Ketchup and brown mustard
MENU: Oven-Fried Potatoes (page 143) and Colorful Coleslaw
   (page 128) or purchased coleslaw

1. Mix all ingredients except hamburger buns. Shape mixture into 4 patties.
2. Heat grill. Grill patties uncovered about 4 inches from medium heat 14
to 18 minutes, turning once, until no longer pink in center and juice is clear.
Serve on buns.

BLACKENED HAMBURGERS: Substitute 1 tablespoon blackened
seasoning for 4 teaspoons Cajun seasoning. Serve with Bourbon Baked
Beans (page 136) and tossed salad with salad dressing.

AMERICA'S BEST HAMBURGERS   4 hamburgers

1 pound lean ground beef
1 1/2 teaspoons Worcestershire sauce
1 1/2 teaspoons steak sauce
1 teaspoon minced garlic
3/4 teaspoon salt
1/4 teaspoon coarse black pepper
4 hamburger buns
Condiments: Lettuce, sliced tomato, ketchup, mustard, sliced
  onions, and sliced pickles
MENU: Old-Fashioned Potato Salad (page 133) or purchased potato
  salad, tossed salad with salad dressing, and ice cream with Chocolate
  Velvet (page 155)

1. Mix all ingredients except hamburger buns. Shape mixture into 4 patties.
2. Heat grill. Grill patties uncovered about 4 inches from medium heat 14
to 18 minutes, turning once, until no longer pink in center and juice is clear.
Serve on buns.

HAMBURGER PARMESAN   4 servings

1 pound lean ground beef
1 slice bread, torn into small pieces (wheat bread is preferred)
1/3 cup grated Parmesan cheese
1 tablespoon milk
1 egg
1/2 teaspoon salt
1/2 teaspoon coarse black pepper
1 cup spaghetti sauce
MENU: Basil-Garlic Mashed Potatoes (page 145) and carrots

1. Mix all ingredients except spaghetti sauce. Shape mixture into 4 patties.
2. Spray a large skillet with nonstick cooking spray; heat skillet over
medium-high heat. Add patties; reduce heat to medium. Cook 10 to 12
minutes, turning once, until no longer pink in center and juices are clear.
Drain.
3. Stir in spaghetti sauce. Cook until hot.

RANCH HOUSE BEEF AND BEANS   4 servings

8 slices turkey bacon
1/2 pound lean ground beef
1/2 cup chopped onion
1 teaspoon minced garlic
1/2 teaspoon salt
1/4 teaspoon coarse black pepper
1 can (15 to 16 ounces) black beans, rinsed and drained
1 can (15 to 16 ounces) red kidney beans, rinsed and drained
1 jar (24 ounces) salsa
Hot dog or hamburger buns
Condiments: Chopped onion and shredded Cheddar cheese
MENU: Chili-Flavored Oven-Fried Potatoes (page 143) and coleslaw

1. Fry bacon in large skillet until brown and crisp. Drain. Tear into small pieces; set aside.
2. Heat skillet over medium-high heat. Cook beef, stirring frequently, until beef is no longer pink; drain. Stir in onion and garlic. Cook until onion is crisp-tender.
3. Stir in bacon pieces and remaining ingredients except buns. Heat to boiling; reduce heat to low. Simmer uncovered 5 minutes, stirring occasionally. Spoon mixture over buns. Top with chopped onion and shredded cheese, if desired.

TEX-MEX SLOPPY JOES   4 servings

1 pound lean ground beef
1 can (10 ounces) diced tomatoes and green chiles (Rotel® is
    preferred)
1 can (8 ounces) tomato sauce
1 teaspoon minced garlic
1/4 to 1/2 teaspoon salt
1/2 teaspoon chili powder
1/2 teaspoon ground cumin
4 hamburger buns
Condiment: Shredded Monterey Jack cheese
MENU: Oven-Fried Potatoes (page 143) and Carrot-Apple Salad
    (page 127)

1. Cook beef in large skillet over medium-high heat, stirring occasionally, until beef is brown; drain.
2. Stir in remaining ingredients except buns. Simmer uncovered 15 to 20 minutes or until sauce is thickened.
3. Fill buns with beef mixture. Top with shredded cheese, if desired.

MEXICAN MEAT LOAF   4 servings

Salsa Ketchup (below)
Meat loaf:
1 pound lean ground beef
1/4 cup ketchup
2 slices bread, torn into small pieces (wheat bread is preferred)
1 egg
1 1/2 teaspoons chili powder
1 1/2 teaspoons ground cumin
3/4 teaspoon salt
MENU: Santa Fe Rice (page 147) and zucchini

1. Heat oven to 375°. Line an 8 1/2-inch loaf dish with aluminum foil, letting aluminum foil extend above pan on 2 sides. Spray with nonstick cooking spray.
2. Mix all meat loaf ingredients. Spread mixture into dish. Bake uncovered 1 hour or until instant-read thermometer reads 160°.
3. Let stand 5 minutes. Lift meat loaf out of dish onto serving platter and peel back aluminum foil from the sides before cutting. Serve with Salsa Ketchup.

SALSA KETCHUP   3/4 cup

1/2 cup salsa
1/4 cup ketchup

Mix salsa and ketchup.

SOUTHWESTERN-STYLE MEATBALLS

3 1/2 to 4 dozen
1-inch meatballs

1 pound lean ground beef
2 slices bread, torn into small pieces (wheat bread is preferred)
1/4 cup tomato juice
1 egg
1 teaspoon chili powder
1 teaspoon ground cumin
1 teaspoon minced garlic
3/4 teaspoon salt
1/4 teaspoon coarse black pepper

1. Mix all ingredients. Shape mixture into 1-inch meatballs.
2. Spray a large skillet with nonstick cooking spray; heat skillet over medium heat. Cook meatballs in cooking spray 10 to 15 minutes, turning occasionally, until meatballs are no longer pink in center. Drain.

SOUTHWESTERN-STYLE COCKTAIL MEATBALLS: Shape Southwestern-Style Meatballs into 3/4-inch meatballs not 1-inch meatballs. Use toothpick to dip meatballs into your favorite salsa or picante sauce.

SOUTHWESTERN-STYLE SPAGHETTI AND MEATBALLS

2 servings

1/2 pound cooked Southwestern-Style Meatballs (above)
Southwestern-Style Tomato Sauce:
1 can (14 1/2 ounces) whole tomatoes, drained
1 can (8 ounces) tomato sauce
1/4 cup vegetable oil
1 to 2 tablespoons canned chopped green chiles
1 teaspoon chili powder
1 teaspoon ground cumin
1 teaspoon minced garlic
1/4 teaspoon salt
1/4 teaspoon coarse black pepper

SHORTCUT:
Substitute 1 1/2 cups picante sauce or salsa for Southwestern-Style Tomato Sauce, if desired.

MENU: Spaghetti, Tossed Salad with Shredded Cheese (page 122) and salad dressing, and toasted French bread

Coarsely chop tomatoes and drain. Mix tomatoes and remaining ingredients except meatballs in large saucepan. Heat to boiling; reduce heat to low. Simmer uncovered 15 minutes, stirring occasionally. Stir in cooked meatballs. Heat until hot. Serve sauce over spaghetti.

HAM-MUSHROOM MANICOTTI   4 servings

3/4 cup spaghetti sauce
6 to 8 cooked manicotti shells
Filling:
3/4 cup low-fat cottage cheese, drained
1/2 cup cubed fully cooked ham
1/2 cup canned mushroom stems and pieces, drained
1/3 cup cubed mozzarella cheese
1/3 cup grated Parmesan cheese
1 medium clove garlic, minced
1 teaspoon dried parsley flakes
1 egg
1/4 teaspoon salt
1/4 teaspoon coarse black pepper
Condiment: Spaghetti sauce
Garnish: Sliced mozzarella cheese and mushroom pieces
MENU: Tossed salad with salad dressing and breadsticks

1. Heat oven to 375°. Line an 11x7x2-inch baking dish with aluminum foil and spray with nonstick cooking spray. Spread half of the spaghetti sauce in dish.
2. Mix all filling ingredients. Fill cooked manicotti shells with cottage cheese mixture. Place shells on spaghetti sauce. Pour remaining spaghetti sauce evenly over shells, covering shells completely.
3. Cover and bake 25 minutes. Top shells with sliced cheese; sprinkle with mushroom pieces. Bake uncovered 5 minutes longer or until cheese is melted. Let stand 5 minutes before serving.

SPAGHETTI WITH HAM-TOMATO SAUCE

2 servings

1 can (14 1/2 ounces) whole tomatoes, drained
1 can (8 ounces) tomato sauce
1 can (4 ounces) sliced mushrooms, drained
1/4 cup vegetable oil
1 tablespoon tomato paste
1 teaspoon minced garlic
1 teaspoon dried parsley flakes
1 teaspoon dried basil leaves
1/2 teaspoon dried thyme leaves
1/4 teaspoon salt
1/4 teaspoon coarse black pepper
1 cup cubed fully cooked ham
MENU: Spaghetti, green beans, and French bread

1. Coarsely chop tomatoes and drain. Mix tomatoes and remaining ingredients except ham in large saucepan. Heat to boiling; reduce heat to low. Simmer uncovered 15 to 20 minutes.
2. Stir in ham. Cook and stir until heated through. Serve sauce over spaghetti.

GRILLED HAM WITH HONEY SALSA

4 servings

1 pound fully cooked ham slice, 1/2- to 3/4-inch thick
Vegetable oil
Honey Salsa:
1 1/2 cups salsa
2 tablespoons honey
MENU: Refried beans, tossed salad with salad dressing, and Herb Corn
  Bread (page 36)

1. Heat grill. Brush ham with oil. Cook ham until heated through, turning once.
2. While ham cooks, mix salsa and honey. Heat salsa mixture on stovetop or in microwave, if desired. Serve ham with sauce.

GRILLED HAM WITH HONEY MUSTARD: Substitute Honey Mustard for Honey Salsa. Mix 1/4 cup honey and 1/4 cup Dijon mustard or brown mustard. Heat mixture on stovetop or in microwave, if desired. Serve with Old-Fashioned Potato Salad (page 133), coleslaw, and Butterscotch-Pecan Apple Pie (page 172).

PORK FAJITAS   4 servings

2 tablespoons vegetable oil, divided
1 medium green bell pepper, cut into 1/4-inch strips
1 medium red bell pepper, cut into 1/4-inch strips
1 medium onion, cut into eighths
2 teaspoons minced garlic, divided
1 pound pork tenderloin, cut into 1/2-inch strips (about 2 cups)
3 tablespoons orange juice
3 tablespoons white vinegar
1 teaspoon chili powder
1 teaspoon ground cumin
1/2 teaspoon salt
1/4 teaspoon coarse black pepper
Flour tortillas (6 to 8 inches in diameter)
Condiments: Salsa, sour cream, guacamole, and jalapeños
MENU: Frijoles Picante (page 136), Santa Fe Rice (page 147), and
 Mexican Sundaes (page 157)

1. Heat 1 tablespoon oil in large skillet over medium-high heat. Cook peppers, onion, and 1 teaspoon garlic in oil, stirring occasionally, until crisp-tender. Remove vegetables from skillet; keep warm.
2. Add remaining 1 tablespoon oil to skillet; heat over medium-high heat. Cook pork and remaining 1 teaspoon garlic in oil 5 to 7 minutes, stirring occasionally, until brown.
3. While pork is cooking, mix orange juice, vinegar, chili powder, cumin, salt, and pepper. Stir orange juice mixture into skillet after pork is brown. Cook over medium heat, stirring constantly, until liquid evaporates.
4. For each fajita, place a few strips of pork, some pepper mixture, and desired condiments on tortilla; roll up.

PORK PICCATA   4 servings

1 pound pork tenderloin, cut into 1/4-inch slices
2 teaspoons lemon pepper
3 tablespoons butter
1/4 to 1/3 cup chicken bouillon
MENU 1: Hamburger buns or rolls, split and toasted, Thyme Oven-
   Fried Potatoes (page 143), and Italian-Style Tossed Salad (page 123)
   with salad dressing
MENU 2: Spaghetti, asparagus, and French bread

1. Sprinkle pork with lemon pepper.
2. Melt butter in large skillet over medium heat. Cook pork in butter 4 to 6
minutes, turning once, until pork is brown. Stir in bouillon; cook over
medium heat 3 minutes, or until mixture is thickened and pork is slightly
pink in center.
3. Serve on a bun for an open-face sandwich (Menu 1) or over spaghetti
(Menu 2).

SLOW COOKER PORK CHALUPAS   4 servings

2 pound pork tenderloin, cut into 1-inch pieces (4 cups)
2 cans (15 to 16 ounces each) red kidney beans, rinsed and drained
1 can (8 ounces) tomato sauce
1/4 cup canned chopped green chiles
4 large cloves garlic, minced
2 tablespoons white vinegar
5 teaspoons chili powder
5 teaspoons ground cumin
2 teaspoons dried oregano leaves
1 teaspoon salt
1/2 teaspoon coarse black pepper
Flour tortillas (6 to 8 inches in diameter)
Condiments: Sour cream, chopped onion, chopped tomatoes, shredded
   Cheddar cheese
MENU: Rice, tossed salad with salad dressing, and Mexican Chocolate
   Chip Cookies (page 161)

1. Spray slow cooker and underside of lid with nonstick cooking spray.
2. Place pork in slow cooker. Mix all remaining ingredients except tortillas; pour mixture over pork. Do not stir.
3. Cover and cook on low setting 8 to 9 hours. Do not remove lid during cooking.
4. Place tortillas on individual serving plates. Spoon pork mixture over tortillas. Top with desired condiments.

ITALIAN BREADED PORK TENDERLOIN

4 servings

2 tablespoons grated Parmesan cheese
2 tablespoons Italian bread crumbs
1/2 teaspoon Italian seasoning
1 pound pork tenderloin
Salt and pepper
Condiment: Spaghetti sauce
MENU: Pesto Rice (page 150) and tossed salad with salad dressing

1. Heat oven to 375°. Line a shallow baking pan with aluminum foil and spray with nonstick cooking spray.
2. Mix Parmesan cheese, Italian bread crumbs, and Italian seasoning.
3. Spray pork with nonstick cooking spray. Sprinkle with salt and pepper. Coat with desired amount of Parmesan cheese mixture. Place in pan. If thicker coating is desired, spray pork with nonstick cooking spray and coat with additional Parmesan cheese mixture.
4. Roast uncovered 50 to 60 minutes or until instant-read thermometer reads 160°. Pork will be slightly pink in the center. Let stand 5 minutes. Cut pork into thin slices.

CUBAN-STYLE ROAST PORK   4 servings

1 pound pork tenderloin
1 medium clove garlic, cut into slivers
1 teaspoon ground cumin
1/2 teaspoon dried oregano leaves
1/2 teaspoon salt
1/2 teaspoon coarse black pepper
MENU: Rice and Black Beans (page 148) and Squash-Tomato Medley
  (page 153)

1. Heat oven to 375°. Line a shallow baking pan with aluminum foil and spray with nonstick cooking spray.
2. Cut slits in pork using a sharp knife; insert garlic slivers. Mix cumin, oregano, salt, and pepper; rub mixture into pork. Place in pan.
3. Roast uncovered 50 to 60 minutes or until instant-read thermometer reads 160°. Pork will be slightly pink in the center. Let stand 5 minutes. Cut pork into thin slices.

CUBAN SANDWICHES   4 servings

Mustard Butter:
1/2 cup butter, softened
1/4 cup prepared mustard
Sandwich:
8 slices bread
1/2 pound Cuban-Style Roast Pork (above), thinly sliced
4 ounces fully cooked smoked ham, thinly sliced
5 to 6 ounces Swiss cheese, thinly sliced
Sandwich-sliced Kosher dill pickles
MENU: Mexican Pasta Salad (page 130) and tossed salad with Creamy
  Caesar Salad Dressing (page 120) or purchased salad dressing

1. Beat butter and mustard until smooth.
2. Spread desired amount of Mustard Butter over one side of each bread slice. Top 4 bread slices, buttered side up, with layers of desired amounts

of pork, ham, Swiss cheese, and pickles. Top with remaining bread slices, buttered side down, pressing firmly to adhere.

3. Heat a griddle over medium heat. Cook sandwiches uncovered about 5 minutes or until bottoms are brown. Turn and cook 3 to 4 minutes or until bottoms are brown and cheese is melted.

POLENTA WITH SAUSAGE-PEPPER SAUCE

4 servings

1/2 pound turkey kielbasa, cut into 1/4-inch slices (about 1 1/3 cups)
1 can (14 1/2 ounces) whole tomatoes, drained
1 can (8 ounces) tomato sauce
1/4 cup olive oil
1 small red bell pepper, cut into 1/4-inch strips
1 small green bell pepper, cut into 1/4-inch strips
1 teaspoon minced garlic
1 teaspoon dried basil leaves
1 teaspoon dried oregano leaves
1 teaspoon sugar
1/4 teaspoon salt
1/4 teaspoon coarse black pepper
Garnish: Shredded Parmesan cheese
MENU: Polenta (page 142) or prepared polenta and tossed salad with
   salad dressing

1. Spray a large saucepan with nonstick cooking spray; heat over medium-high heat. Cook kielbasa in nonstick cooking spray 8 to 10 minutes, stirring occasionally, until brown.

2. Coarsely chop tomatoes and drain. Add tomatoes and remaining ingredients to saucepan; stir to combine. Heat to boiling; reduce heat to low. Simmer uncovered 20 minutes, stirring occasionally. Serve sauce over polenta; garnish with Parmesan cheese.

POLENTA WITH SAUSAGE-MUSHROOM SAUCE: Substitute
1/2 pound sliced mushrooms (about 3 cups) for red bell pepper and green bell pepper.

ITALIAN MEATBALLS   3 1/2 to 4 dozen 1-inch meatballs

1 pound turkey sausage
2 slices bread, torn into small pieces (wheat bread is preferred)
1 egg
2 teaspoons dried parsley flakes
1 teaspoon minced garlic

1. Mix all ingredients. Shape mixture into 1-inch meatballs.
2. Spray a large skillet with nonstick cooking spray; heat over medium heat. Cook meatballs in cooking spray 10 to 15 minutes, turning occasionally, until meatballs are no longer pink in center. Drain. These versatile meatballs are delicious additions to sauces, soups, and pizza. They can be frozen.

ITALIAN COCKTAIL MEATBALLS: Shape Italian Meatballs into 3/4-inch meatballs instead of 1-inch meatballs. Use toothpicks to dip meatballs into your favorite spaghetti sauce.

MEATBALLS AND RED PEPPER-   2 servings
BLACK OLIVE SAUCE

1/2 pound cooked Italian Meatballs (above or purchased meatballs)
Red Pepper-Black Olive Sauce:
1 can (14 1/2 ounces) whole tomatoes, drained
1 can (8 ounces) tomato sauce
1/2 cup chopped red bell pepper
1/2 cup halved black olives
1/4 cup olive oil
1 teaspoon minced garlic
1 teaspoon dried parsley flakes
1 teaspoon Italian seasoning
1/4 teaspoon salt
1/4 teaspoon coarse black pepper
1/16 to 1/4 teaspoon red pepper flakes
MENU: Spaghetti, tossed salad with salad dressing, and Thyme Bread
   (page 46)

Coarsely chop tomatoes and drain. Mix tomatoes and remaining ingredients except meatballs in large saucepan. Heat to boiling; reduce heat to low. Simmer uncovered 20 minutes. Stir in meatballs. Cook uncovered over medium heat until heated through. Serve sauce over spaghetti.

MEATBALLS AND TETRAZINI SAUCE

2 servings

1/2 pound cooked Italian Meatballs (page 106 or purchased meatballs)
Tetrazini Sauce:
1 cup White Sauce (page 117 or prepared white sauce)
1/2 cup grated Parmesan cheese
1/4 cup white wine
1 can (4 ounces) sliced mushrooms, drained
1 teaspoon dried parsley flakes
1 medium clove garlic, minced
1/2 bay leaf, crumbled
1/2 teaspoon chicken bouillon granules
1/4 teaspoon coarse black pepper
MENU: Spaghetti, Italian-Style Tossed Salad (page 123) with salad
   dressing, and French bread

1. Mix white sauce and remaining ingredients except meatballs in large saucepan. Heat to boiling; reduce heat to low. Simmer uncovered 5 minutes, stirring occasionally, until cheese is melted and sauce is smooth.
2. Stir in meatballs. Cook uncovered over medium heat until heated through. Serve sauce over spaghetti.

ITALIAN HERB MEAT LOAF   4 servings

1 pound lean ground turkey
2 slices bread, torn into small pieces (wheat bread is preferred)
1 egg
1/2 cup chopped onion
1/4 cup chopped green bell pepper
1/4 cup chopped red bell pepper
1/4 cup ketchup
3 tablespoons grated Parmesan cheese
1 teaspoon minced garlic
3/4 teaspoon salt
1/2 teaspoon dried basil leaves
1/2 teaspoon dried oregano leaves
1/2 teaspoon dried parsley flakes
1/4 teaspoon coarse black pepper
Condiment: Spaghetti sauce
MENU: Spaghetti and green beans

1. Heat oven to 350°. Line an 8 1/2-inch loaf dish with aluminum foil, letting aluminum foil extend above pan on 2 sides. Spray with nonstick cooking spray.
2. Mix all ingredients. Spread mixture into dish.
3. Bake 50 to 60 minutes or until instant-read thermometer reads 180°. Let stand 5 minutes. Lift meat loaf out of dish onto serving platter and peel back aluminum foil from the sides before cutting. Serve with spaghetti sauce.

PAPRIKA BREADED   4 servings
TURKEY CUTLETS

1 pound turkey breast slices, pounded to even thickness
Butter-flavored nonstick cooking spray
Salt and pepper
1 cup soft bread crumbs (wheat bread is preferred)
2 tablespoons grated Parmesan cheese
1 teaspoon paprika
Condiment: Spaghetti sauce
MENU: Italian-Style Rice and Vegetables (page 150) and shredded
   carrots served on salad greens with salad dressing

1. Heat oven to 375°. Line a shallow baking pan with aluminum foil and spray with nonstick cooking spray.

2. Spray turkey with butter-flavored nonstick cooking spray; sprinkle with salt and pepper. Mix bread crumbs, Parmesan cheese, and paprika. Coat turkey with bread crumb mixture, pressing to adhere. Place in pan.

3. Bake 20 to 22 minutes or until turkey is no longer pink in the center.

TURKEY FAJITAS   4 servings

1 tablespoon vegetable oil
1 pound turkey tenderloin, cut into 1-inch pieces (about 2 cups)
2 large cloves garlic, minced
1 to 1 1/4 teaspoons chili powder
1 to 1 1/4 teaspoons ground cumin
3/4 teaspoon dried oregano leaves
1/2 teaspoon salt
1/4 teaspoon coarse black pepper
2 tablespoons canned chopped green chiles
3 tablespoons orange juice
3 tablespoons white vinegar
Flour tortillas (6 to 8 inches in diameter)
Condiments: Salsa, guacamole, and sour cream
MENU: Mexican Refried Beans (page 137) and Chicken-Flavored Rice
   (page 151)

1. Heat oil in large skillet over medium-high heat. Cook turkey and garlic in oil until brown on all sides, stirring frequently.

2. Stir in remaining ingredients except tortillas. Heat to boiling; reduce heat to low. Simmer uncovered 3 to 5 minutes or until turkey is no longer pink when cut.

3. For each fajita, place turkey, sauce, and desired condiments on tortilla; roll up.

TURKEY IN ORIENTAL SAUCE   4 servings

Oriental Sauce (below)
1 pound turkey tenderloin, cut into 1-inch pieces (about 2 cups)
Salt and pepper
2 tablespoons vegetable oil, divided
1 small red bell pepper, cut into 1/4-inch strips
1 small green bell pepper, cut into 1/4-inch strips
2 medium stalks celery, cut into 1/4-inch strips (same length as
    peppers)
1 small onion, cut into eighths
MENU: Rice

1. Prepare Oriental Sauce; keep warm.
2. Sprinkle turkey with salt and pepper. Heat 1 tablespoon oil in large skillet over medium-high heat. Cook turkey in oil 5 to 7 minutes, stirring frequently, until turkey is no longer pink when cut. Remove from skillet with slotted spoon; keep warm.
3. Add remaining 1 tablespoon oil to skillet. Heat over medium-high heat. Add peppers, celery, and onion. Stir-fry 3 to 5 minutes or until vegetables are crisp-tender. Stir in drained turkey and Oriental Sauce. Cook over medium heat until heated through. Serve over rice.

ORIENTAL SAUCE   about 1 1/2 cups

1 1/2 to 2 tablespoons cornstarch
1/2 teaspoon chicken bouillon granules
1/2 teaspoon MSG
1 cup water
1/4 cup soy sauce
1/4 cup dry sherry

Mix cornstarch, chicken bouillon granules, and MSG in small saucepan. Gradually stir in water, soy sauce, and sherry. Cook over medium heat, stirring frequently, until sauce is thickened.

SANTA FE ROAST TURKEY   4 servings

3-pound boneless turkey
3/4 teaspoon chili powder
3/4 teaspoon ground cumin
3/4 teaspoon rubbed sage
1/2 teaspoon salt
1/2 teaspoon coarse black pepper
Condiment: Cranberry Salsa (below)
MENU: Southwestern Succotash (page 152), Santa Fe Rice (page 147), and New Mexican Corn Bread (page 36)

1. Heat oven to 325°. Line a shallow baking pan with aluminum foil and spray with nonstick cooking spray.
2. Remove netting from turkey. Mix chili powder, cumin, sage, salt, and pepper. Rub chili powder mixture into turkey. Place in pan.
3. Roast 1 hour 45 minutes to 2 hours 15 minutes or until instant-read thermometer reads 170° and juice of turkey is no longer pink when cut. Remove from oven. Cover turkey loosely with tent of aluminum foil. Let stand 15 minutes for easiest carving. Serve turkey with Cranberry Salsa.

CRANBERRY SALSA   1 1/2 cups

1 cup salsa
1/2 cup whole berry cranberry sauce

Mix salsa and whole berry cranberry sauce. Serve room temperature or chilled.

MIX-AND-MATCH CASSEROLE   4 servings

Assemble a delicious casserole based on ingredients you have on hand. Select ingredients from each category.

STARCH: 2 cups cooked rice (white long grain, brown rice, or wild rice) or 2 cups cooked pasta (spaghetti, macaroni, egg noodles, rigatoni, or rotini)

SAUCE: 1 can (10 3/4 ounces) condensed cream-style soup, tomato soup, or cheddar cheese soup, 1 1/2 to 2 cups spaghetti sauce, salsa, picante sauce, white sauce, or Alfredo Sauce

MEAT (COOKED): 1 cup chopped chicken, turkey, beef, ham, or pork, 1 cup ground beef, turkey, or pork (drained), 1 cup pork or turkey sausage (drained), 1 cup sliced kielbasa sausage, smoked sausage, or hot dogs, 6 to 8 slices bacon or turkey bacon, crumbled, 1 can (6 ounces) tuna, drained and flaked), or 1 can (6 ounces) salmon, drained

VEGETABLE (COOKED): (Use 1 vegetable or a combination to equal 1 cup. Drain canned vegetables.) black beans, broccoli florets, green beans, mixed vegetables, sliced mushrooms, green peas, red kidney beans, whole kernel corn, cubed or sliced zucchini or yellow squash

EXTRA FLAVOR: (Choose 1 or 2 ingredients, using 1/2 cup each) chopped green or red bell pepper, green onion, onion, or celery, sliced water chestnuts, chopped or sliced black olives

SEASONING: (Add 1 or more ingredients, if desired) 1 teaspoon minced garlic, 2 to 4 tablespoons canned chopped green chiles, 1/2 to 1 teaspoon purchased seasoning mix (such as Cajun or Jerk), 1/2 to 1 teaspoon dried herb (basil, dill weed, oregano, parsley, Italian seasoning, or thyme), 1/2 to 1 teaspoon curry powder, or 1/2 teaspoon black pepper

TOPPING: 1/2 to 1 cup shredded Cheddar, Monterey Jack, Monterey Jack with jalapeños, Swiss, Colby, or Muenster cheese (2 to 4 ounces), 1/4 cup grated Parmesan cheese, 1/4 cup soft bread crumbs, or 1 slice bread, cut into cubes

MENU: Tossed salad with salad dressing and rolls

1. Heat oven to 375°. Line an 11x7x2-inch baking dish with aluminum foil; spray with nonstick cooking spray.
2. Select ingredients from each category except topping; mix ingredients in large bowl. Taste mixture and increase the quantity of favorite ingredients, if desired. If mixture is too thick, thin with additional sauce, milk, or tomato juice. Spread in pan. Sprinkle with a topping.
3. Bake uncovered 25 to 30 minutes or until hot.

ITALIAN WEDDING SOUP   2 servings

1/2 pound cooked Italian Meatballs (page 106) or purchased meatballs
1 can (14 ounces) chicken broth
1/2 cup cooked rice
1 teaspoon dried parsley flakes
1 large clove garlic, minced
1/4 teaspoon coarse black pepper
2 tablespoons grated Parmesan cheese
MENU: Carrot and celery sticks and Parmesan Corn Bread (page 36)

Heat all ingredients except Parmesan cheese in large saucepan to boiling;
reduce heat to low. Simmer uncovered 10 minutes. Stir in Parmesan cheese;
serve immediately.

TORTILLA SOUP   4 servings

1 can (14 1/2 ounces) whole tomatoes
3/4 cup chopped onion
2 large cloves garlic, minced
1 can (14 ounces) beef broth
1 1/2 cups shredded cooked chicken
1 tablespoon tomato paste
1 tablespoon dried parsley flakes
1 teaspoon chili powder
1 teaspoon ground cumin
1 beef bouillon cube
1/2 teaspoon Worcestershire sauce
1/4 teaspoon salt
1/4 teaspoon coarse black pepper
Garnish: Baked Corn Tortilla Strips (page 39), sour cream, and
   chopped avocado
MENU: Tossed Salad with Shredded Cheese (page 122) and salad
   dressing

1. Place tomatoes, onion, and garlic in blender. Cover and blend on high
speed until smooth, scraping down sides if necessary.
2. Pour tomato mixture into large saucepan. Stir in remaining ingredients.
Heat to boiling; reduce heat to low. Cover and simmer 20 minutes. Top each
serving with tortilla strips, sour cream, and chopped avocado.

113

PICANTE CHILI   4 servings

1 pound lean ground beef
1 cup chopped onion
1 teaspoon minced garlic
1 can (14 1/2 ounces) whole tomatoes
1 jar (16 ounces) picante sauce
1 can (16 ounces) red kidney beans
2 cans (8 ounces each) tomato sauce
2 teaspoons dried parsley flakes
MENU: Corn-on-the-Cobb with Mexican Butter (page 138) and
    Corn Bread Waffles (page 32) or Corn Bread (page 36)

1. Cook beef in large skillet over medium-high heat, stirring occasionally, until beef is brown; drain. Add onion and garlic; cook until onion is crisp-tender. Place beef mixture in stockpot.
2. Coarsely chop tomatoes, reserving juice. Add tomatoes, tomato juice, and remaining ingredients to stockpot; stir to combine. Heat to boiling; reduce heat to low. Cover and simmer 25 minutes, stirring occasionally.

WHITE CHILI   4 servings

1 teaspoon vegetable oil
1 cup chopped onion
1 teaspoon minced garlic
2 cans (14 ounces each) chicken broth
2 cups cut-up cooked chicken breasts
1 can (15 1/2 ounces) navy beans
1 to 2 tablespoons canned chopped green chiles
1 1/2 teaspoons ground cumin
1 teaspoon dried oregano leaves
1/2 to 3/4 teaspoon white pepper or coarse black pepper
3/4 teaspoon salt
Garnish: Shredded Monterey Jack cheese, sour cream, and jalapeños
MENU: Coleslaw and flour tortillas with butter

1. Heat oil in a stockpot on medium-high heat. Cook onion and garlic in oil until crisp-tender. Stir in remaining ingredients. Heat to boiling; reduce heat to low. Cover and simmer 15 minutes, stirring occasionally.
2. Ladle soup into bowls and garnish with cheese, sour cream, and jalapeños.

RED CHICKEN CHILI   4 servings

2 teaspoons vegetable oil
1 cup chopped onion
1 teaspoon minced garlic
1 can (14 1/2 ounces) whole tomatoes
1 can (14 ounces) chicken broth
2 cups cut-up cooked chicken
1 can (15 to 16 ounces) red kidney beans
1 can (8 ounces) tomato sauce
2 teaspoons chili powder
2 teaspoons ground cumin
1/2 teaspoon dried oregano leaves
1/4 teaspoon salt
1/4 teaspoon coarse black pepper
Garnish: Sour cream and cubed avocado
MENU: Tossed salad with salad dressing and Corn Bread (page 36)

1. Heat oil in a stockpot. Cook onion and garlic in oil, stirring frequently, until crisp-tender.
2. Coarsely chop tomatoes, reserving juice. Add tomatoes, tomato juice, and remaining ingredients to stockpot; stir to combine. Heat to boiling; reduce heat to low. Cover and simmer 30 minutes, stirring occasionally.
3. Ladle soup into bowls and garnish with dollop of sour cream and cubed avocado.

MEXICAN REFRIED BEAN SOUP   4 servings

1 can (14 1/2 ounces) whole tomatoes
1 can (14 ounces) beef broth
1 can (16 ounces) refried beans
1/2 cup chopped onion
1/2 cup chopped celery
1 large clove garlic, minced
Garnish: Shredded Cheddar cheese or Monterey Jack cheese
MENU: Salsa Slaw (page 128) or purchased coleslaw and flour tortillas

Coarsely chop tomatoes, reserving juice. Mix tomatoes, tomato juice, and remaining ingredients in large saucepan. Heat to boiling; reduce heat to low. Cover and simmer 20 minutes. Top each serving with cheese.

TEXAS-STYLE ONION SOUP   2 servings

2 tablespoons butter
1 large onion, thinly sliced and separated into rings
1 teaspoon minced garlic
1 cup tomato juice
1 can (14 ounces) beef broth
1/4 cup picante sauce
1/4 teaspoon coarse black pepper
Garnish: Cheddar cheese or Colby cheese, cut into cubes
MENU: Mexican Refried Bean Toast (page 137) and coleslaw

1. Melt butter in nonstick stockpot over medium heat. Cook onion in butter until crisp-tender, about 10 minutes, stirring constantly.
2. Stir in remaining ingredients. Heat to boiling; reduce heat to low. Simmer uncovered 10 minutes.
3. Ladle soup into bowls. Sprinkle cheese cubes over soup.

SALMON CHOWDER   4 servings

1 tablespoon butter
1 medium potato, cubed (1 cup)
1/2 cup chopped onion
1 can (14 1/2 ounces) whole tomatoes
1 can (10 3/4 ounces) condensed cream of potato soup
3/4 cup milk
1 teaspoon dried parsley flakes
1/2 teaspoon Worcestershire sauce
1/2 teaspoon dried thyme leaves
1/2 teaspoon salt
1/4 teaspoon coarse black pepper
1 can (6 1/8 ounces) salmon, drained and skin removed
MENU: Tossed salad with salad dressing and Oat Bran English Muffin
    Bread (page 47) or purchased English muffins with butter

1. Melt butter in nonstick stockpot over medium heat. Cook potatoes in butter 5 minutes, stirring occasionally. Stir in onion. Cook until potatoes and onion are crisp-tender, about 2 minutes.
2. Coarsely chop tomatoes, reserving juice. Add tomatoes, tomato juice, and remaining ingredients, except salmon, to stockpot; stir to combine. Heat uncovered until hot. Do not boil. Stir in salmon; cook until heated through.

EASY CHEESY SAUCE   about 2/3 cup

3 to 4 tablespoons milk, divided
5 slices process American cheese, torn into pieces

1. Place 2 tablespoons milk and cheese pieces in microwavable bowl. Cover loosely with plastic wrap. Heat in microwave on High (100%), stopping and stirring, until melted and completely smooth.
2. Gradually stir in 1 to 2 tablespoons milk to thin. Cover loosely with plastic wrap; heat on High (100%) 5 to 10 seconds. Serve with vegetables or fish.

WHITE SAUCE   1 cup

1 tablespoon cornstarch
4 teaspoons flour
1/4 teaspoon salt
3 tablespoons water
1 cup milk

Mix cornstarch, flour, and salt in small saucepan. Stir in water. Gradually stir in milk. Heat over medium heat until mixture thickens, stirring constantly.

ALFREDO SAUCE   1 1/4 cups

1 tablespoon cornstarch
4 teaspoons flour
1/4 teaspoon salt
3 tablespoons water
1 1/4 cups milk
3/4 cup grated Parmesan cheese
1/4 teaspoon minced garlic

1. Mix cornstarch, flour, and salt in small saucepan. Stir in water. Gradually stir in milk. Cook over medium heat, stirring constantly, until mixture thickens.
2. Stir in Parmesan cheese and garlic. Cook over low heat 3 to 5 minutes, stirring constantly, until cheese is melted and mixture is completely smooth.

117

SPAGHETTI SAUCE   about 2 cups

1 can (14 1/2 ounces) whole tomatoes, drained
1 can (8 ounces) tomato sauce
1/2 cup chopped onion
1/4 cup vegetable oil
1 1/2 teaspoons minced garlic
1 teaspoon dried basil leaves
1 teaspoon dried oregano leaves
1 teaspoon dried parsley flakes
1 teaspoon sugar
1/2 teaspoon salt
1/4 teaspoon coarse black pepper

Coarsely chop tomatoes and drain. Mix tomatoes and remaining ingredients in large saucepan. Heat to boiling; reduce heat to low. Simmer uncovered 15 minutes, stirring occasionally.

ENCHILADA SAUCE   about 2 1/2 cups

1 tablespoon vegetable oil
1/2 cup chopped onion
1 cup tomato purée
2 cans (8 ounces each) tomato sauce
2 teaspoons lemon juice
2 teaspoons chili powder
1 1/2 teaspoons ground cumin
1 teaspoon minced garlic
1/2 teaspoon dried oregano leaves
1/4 teaspoon coarse black pepper

1. Heat oil in large saucepan over medium-high heat. Cook onion in oil until crisp-tender.
2. Add tomato purée and remaining ingredients to saucepan, stirring to combine. Heat to boiling; reduce heat to low. Simmer uncovered 10 minutes, stirring occasionally.

5
SIDE DISHES

CRANBERRY-ORANGE RELISH   2 1/2 cups

1 small navel orange
2 cups fresh cranberries
2 large red delicious apples, peeled and chopped (2 cups)
1 cup sugar

1. Zest orange (about 2 teaspoons zest). Peel orange and slice.
2. Place orange zest, orange slices, cranberries, and apples in food processor. Cover and process with short on-and-off motions until evenly chopped. Place cranberry mixture in large glass or plastic bowl; stir in sugar.
3. Cover and refrigerate at least 8 hours to blend flavors. Serve with turkey or chicken.

CRANBERRY WALDORF SALSA   2 cups

1 large unpeeled red delicious apple, chopped (1 cup)
1/2 to 2/3 cup whole berry cranberry sauce
1/3 cup chopped celery
1/4 cup chopped walnuts

Mix all ingredients in large glass or plastic bowl. Serve immediately or cover and refrigerate until ready to serve.

CREAMY CAESAR SALAD DRESSING   2/3 cup

1/2 cup low-fat yogurt
1/4 cup grated Parmesan cheese
2 teaspoons lemon juice
1 teaspoon red wine vinegar
1 teaspoon Dijon mustard
1 teaspoon Worcestershire sauce
1 medium clove garlic, minced
1/8 teaspoon coarse black pepper

Mix all ingredients in small glass or plastic bowl. Serve immediately or cover and refrigerate until ready to serve.

CALIFORNIA-STYLE GARLIC   1/2 cup
SALAD DRESSING

1/2 cup low-fat yogurt
2 tablespoons grated Parmesan cheese
2 teaspoons milk
1/4 teaspoon Italian seasoning
1/4 teaspoon salt
1/4 teaspoon coarse black pepper
1/4 teaspoon McCormick's ® California-Style minced garlic

Mix all ingredients in small glass or plastic bowl. Serve immediately or cover and refrigerate until ready to serve.

PARMESAN SALAD DRESSING   1 cup

1 cup low-fat cottage cheese
1/4 cup grated Parmesan cheese
1 teaspoon coarse black pepper
1 teaspoon white wine vinegar
1/4 teaspoon salt
1 tablespoon milk, if desired

Place all ingredients except milk in food processor. Cover and process until smooth. If a thinner salad dressing is desired, add milk and process until smooth. Place in small glass or plastic bowl. Serve immediately or cover and refrigerate until ready to serve.

PESTO SALAD DRESSING   1 cup

3/4 cup low-fat cottage cheese
1/2 cup packed fresh basil leaves
5 tablespoons grated Parmesan cheese
3 tablespoons milk
2 tablespoons chopped green onion
1/4 teaspoon salt
1/4 teaspoon coarse black pepper

Place all ingredients in food processor. Cover and process until smooth. Place in small glass or plastic bowl. Serve immediately or cover and refrigerate until ready to serve.

LOW-FAT RANCH SALAD DRESSING   1/2 cup

1/2 cup low-fat yogurt
1 to 2 teaspoons dry ranch salad dressing mix

Mix yogurt and salad dressing mix in small glass or plastic bowl. Serve immediately or cover and refrigerate until ready to serve.

LOW-FAT TACO SALAD DRESSING: Substitute 1 to 2 teaspoons dry taco seasoning mix for ranch salad dressing mix.

CRISPY CROUTONS

Butter-flavored or olive oil-flavored nonstick cooking spray
Dry French or Italian bread*, cut into 1 1/2-inch cubes
Salt or seasoned salt

1. Spray a skillet with nonstick cooking spray. Heat over medium heat. Add bread cubes to skillet; lightly spray with nonstick cooking spray. Cook bread cubes in cooking spray over medium heat about 5 minutes, stirring frequently, until golden brown. Sprinkle with salt.
2. Remove croutons from skillet. Cool on wire rack. Serve with salads or soups.

*Substitute breads (pages 46, 47) or corn bread (page 36), if desired.

EXTRA-CRISPY CROUTONS
1. Heat oven to 400°. Line a shallow baking pan with aluminum foil.
2. Prepare Crispy Croutons as directed in Step #1. Place croutons in pan. Bake 5 to 8 minutes or until very brown and crisp.
3. Remove croutons from pan. Cool on wire rack.

TOSSED SALAD WITH SHREDDED CHEESE

2 servings

4 cups bite-size pieces mixed salad greens
1/4 cup chopped green onions
1/4 cup shredded Cheddar cheese
1/4 cup shredded Monterey Jack cheese
2 slices bacon, crisply cooked and crumbed
10 pitted black olives, halved
Garnish: 1/2 medium red bell pepper, cut into 1/4-inch strips
Serve with: Salad dressing

Place salad greens in individual serving bowls. Sprinkle remaining ingredients over salad greens in order listed. Garnish rim of bowls with red pepper strips. Serve with salad dressing.

ITALIAN-STYLE TOSSED SALAD   4 servings

8 cups bite-size pieces mixed salad greens
4 radishes, sliced
1/2 cup chopped green onions
16 to 20 pitted black olives, halved
16 cherry tomatoes, halved
8 whole mushrooms, sliced
Garnish: 1 large green bell pepper, cut into 5 rings
Serve with: Salad dressing

Toss salad greens and remaining ingredients in large bowl. Garnish with pepper rings. Serve with salad dressing.

HEARTS OF PALM TOSSED SALAD   4 servings

8 cups bite-size pieces mixed salad greens
1/2 cup chopped green onions
12 canned hearts of palm, drained and split lengthwise
1/4 cup sliced olives
Serve with: Salad dressing

1. Toss salad greens and green onions. Place in 4 individual serving bowls.
2. Arrange hearts of palm in a row over salad greens; sprinkle black olives over hearts of palm. Serve with salad dressing.

GREEK SALAD FOR TWO   2 servings

4 cups bite-size pieces romaine
1 medium tomato, cut into wedges
1/2 medium cucumber, peeled and thinly sliced
1/2 cup crumbed feta cheese (2 ounces)
14 pitted black olives, halved
2 to 3 red onion slices, separated into rings
Serve with: Salad dressing

Toss romaine and remaining ingredients in large bowl. Serve with salad dressing.

MEXICAN-STYLE TOSSED SALAD   4 servings

8 cups bite-size pieces mixed salad greens
1/2 cup chopped green onions
1/2 cup red kidney beans, rinsed and drained
1/2 cup coarsely chopped celery
16 pitted black olives, halved
12 cherry tomatoes, halved
Serve with: Cheese Salad Dressing (page 75) or Low-Fat Taco Salad
    Dressing (page 121)

Toss salad greens and green onions in large bowl. Sprinkle remaining
ingredients over salad greens in order listed. Serve with salad dressing.

HERBED BEAN SALAD   4 servings

1 can (15 ounces) red kidney beans, rinsed and drained
1 can (14 1/2 ounces) cut green beans, drained
1/2 medium onion, thinly sliced and separated into rings
1 jar (4 ounces) chopped pimientos, drained (1/2 cup)
Dressing:
1/3 cup sugar
1/3 cup white vinegar
2 tablespoons vegetable oil
1 teaspoon balsamic vinegar
1 tablespoon dried parsley flakes
1 teaspoon dried basil leaves
1/2 teaspoon dried dill weed
1/4 teaspoon garlic powder
1/4 teaspoon salt
1/4 teaspoon coarse black pepper

1. Mix kidney beans, green beans, onion, and pimientos in large glass or
plastic bowl.
2. Shake all dressing ingredients in tightly covered container. Toss dressing
and kidney bean mixture until evenly coated. Serve immediately or cover
and refrigerate until ready to serve. Serve with slotted spoon.

TWO-BEAN SALAD   4 servings

1 can (15 ounces) red kidney beans, rinsed and drained
1 can (14 1/2 ounces) cut green beans, drained
1/2 cup chopped celery
1/2 cup chopped onion
1/2 cup chopped red bell pepper
Dressing:
1/2 cup sugar
1/2 cup white vinegar
1 tablespoon olive oil
1/4 teaspoon salt
1/4 teaspoon coarse black pepper

1. Mix kidney beans, green beans, celery, onion, and red pepper in large glass or plastic bowl.
2. Shake all dressing ingredients in tightly covered container. Toss dressing and kidney bean mixture until evenly coated. Cover and refrigerate 30 minutes to blend flavors. Serve with slotted spoon.

ITALIAN GREEN BEAN SALAD   4 servings

2 cups cooked Italian green beans or cut green beans
1 can (4 ounces) sliced mushrooms, drained
1/2 cup chopped red bell pepper
1/2 cup halved black olives
2 tablespoons olive oil
1 large clove garlic, minced
1/2 teaspoon Italian seasoning
3/4 teaspoon salt
1/4 teaspoon coarse black pepper
2 tablespoons red wine vinegar

Mix green beans and remaining ingredients except red wine vinegar in large saucepan. Cook until hot. Stir in red wine vinegar. Serve immediately or cover and refrigerate until chilled, if desired.

BLACK BEAN-CORN SALAD   4 servings

1 can (15 ounces) black beans, rinsed and drained
1 can (8 3/4 ounces) whole kernel corn, drained (1 cup)
1/2 cup chopped onion
1 jar (2 ounces) chopped pimientos, drained (1/4 cup)
Dressing:
1/2 cup sugar
1/2 cup white vinegar
1/2 teaspoon celery seed
1/4 teaspoon salt
1/4 teaspoon coarse black pepper

1. Mix black beans, corn, onion, and pimientos in medium glass or plastic bowl.
2. Shake all dressing ingredients in tightly covered container. Toss dressing and black bean mixture until evenly coated. Serve immediately or cover and refrigerate until ready to serve. Serve with slotted spoon.

BLACK BEAN SALAD   4 servings

1 can (14 1/2 ounces) whole tomatoes, drained
1 can (15 to 16 ounces) black beans, drained
1/2 cup chopped onion
2 tablespoons chopped green onion
2 tablespoons canned chopped green chiles
2 tablespoons red wine vinegar
1 large clove garlic, minced
1 teaspoon dried parsley flakes
1/4 teaspoon salt
1/4 teaspoon coarse black pepper

Coarsely chop tomatoes and drain. Mix tomatoes and remaining ingredients in large glass or plastic bowl. Cover and refrigerate 1 hour to blend flavors.

CARROT-APPLE SALAD 2 servings

1 cup shredded carrot (1 medium)
1 large red delicious apple, peeled and shredded (1 cup)
1/2 cup raisins
1/3 cup low-fat yogurt
1 tablespoon salad dressing or mayonnaise, heaping
2 teaspoons sugar
1/8 teaspoon salt

Mix all ingredients in medium glass or plastic bowl. Serve immediately or cover and refrigerate until ready to serve.

CARROT-ZUCCHINI SLAW 2 servings

1 cup shredded zucchini (1 medium)
1 cup shredded carrot (1 medium)
1/3 cup chopped onion
Dressing:
1/4 cup salad dressing or mayonnaise
1/4 cup salsa
1 teaspoon white vinegar
1/4 teaspoon salt
1/4 teaspoon coarse black pepper

1. Mix zucchini, carrot, and onion in medium glass or plastic bowl.
2. Mix all dressing ingredients. Toss dressing and zucchini mixture until evenly coated. Serve immediately or cover and refrigerate until ready to serve.

COLORFUL COLESLAW   4 servings

3 1/2 cups shredded cabbage
1 cup shredded carrot (1 medium)
1/2 cup chopped onion
1/2 cup chopped red bell pepper
1/2 cup chopped green bell pepper
Dressing:
3/4 cup sugar
1/2 cup rice vinegar (4.1% acidity)
2 tablespoons vegetable oil
1/2 teaspoon salt, scant
1/2 teaspoon coarse black pepper

1. Mix cabbage, carrot, onion, and peppers in large glass or plastic bowl.
2. Shake all dressing ingredients in tightly covered container. Toss dressing and cabbage mixture until evenly coated. Cover and refrigerate 1 hour to blend flavors. Serve with slotted spoon.

SALSA SLAW   3 to 4 servings

2 1/2 cups shredded cabbage
1/2 cup shredded carrot (1/2 medium)
1/3 cup chopped green bell pepper
Dressing:
1/2 cup salsa
1/3 cup salad dressing or mayonnaise
1 tablespoon white vinegar
1/4 teaspoon salt
1/4 teaspoon coarse black pepper

1. Mix cabbage, carrot, and green pepper in large glass or plastic bowl.
2. Mix all dressing ingredients. Toss dressing and cabbage mixture until evenly coated. Serve immediately or cover and refrigerate until ready to serve. Serve with slotted spoon.

CORN-TOMATO SALAD   2 servings

1 can (8 3/4 ounces) whole kernel corn, drained (1 cup)
1/2 cup chopped tomato
1/3 cup minced onion
2 tablespoons minced green onion
2 tablespoons lime juice
1 teaspoon dried parsley flakes
1/4 teaspoon salt

Mix all ingredients in medium glass or plastic bowl. Cover and refrigerate 1 hour to blend flavors. Serve with slotted spoon.

GREEK VEGETABLE SALAD   4 servings

1 cup cubed cucumber
1 cup chopped green bell pepper
1 cup chopped red bell pepper
3/4 cup halved black olives
1/2 cup chopped onion
1/2 cup crumbled feta cheese (2 ounces)
2 tablespoons lemon juice
2 tablespoons vegetable oil
1 teaspoon minced garlic
1 teaspoon dried oregano leaves
1 teaspoon dried basil leaves
1 teaspoon dried parsley flakes
1/4 teaspoon salt
1/4 teaspoon coarse black pepper

Mix all ingredients in large glass or plastic bowl. Serve immediately or cover and refrigerate until ready to serve.

MACARONI-OLIVE SALAD   4 servings

2 cups uncooked elbow macaroni (7 ounces)
1/2 cup chopped onion
1/2 cup chopped pimiento-stuffed green olives
1/2 cup halved black olives
4 teaspoons capers, drained
Dressing:
1/2 cup salad dressing or mayonnaise
1/4 cup sour cream
1 tablespoon Dijon mustard
1/2 teaspoon salt
1/4 teaspoon coarse black pepper

1. Cook macaroni as directed on package; rinse and drain. Mix macaroni, onion, green olives, black olives, and capers in large glass or plastic bowl.
2. Mix all dressing ingredients. Toss dressing and macaroni mixture until evenly coated. Cover and refrigerate 1 hour to blend flavors.

MEXICAN PASTA SALAD   4 servings

1 cup uncooked elbow macaroni (3 1/2 ounces)
1/2 cup chopped onion
1/2 cup halved black olives
1/3 cup chopped green bell pepper
1/3 cup chopped red bell pepper
1 can (14 1/2 ounces) whole tomatoes, drained
Dressing:
3 tablespoons white vinegar
2 tablespoons salad dressing or mayonnaise
1 teaspoon minced garlic
1 teaspoon chili powder
1 teaspoon dried parsley flakes
3/4 teaspoon salt
1/4 teaspoon garlic salt
1/4 teaspoon coarse black pepper

1. Cook macaroni as directed on package; rinse and drain. Mix macaroni, onion, black olives, and peppers in large glass or plastic bowl.
2. Chop tomatoes and drain. Place tomatoes in single layer between double layer of paper towels. Press to remove juice. Stir tomatoes into macaroni mixture.
3. Mix all dressing ingredients. Toss dressing and macaroni mixture until evenly coated. Cover and refrigerate 1 hour to blend flavors.

ITALIAN PASTA SALAD   4 servings

1 cup uncooked rotini (corkscrew-shaped pasta)
1 jar (6 ounces) marinated artichoke hearts, drained and coarsely
    chopped
1/2 cup halved black olives
1/2 cup chopped onion
1/2 cup chopped red bell pepper
1/4 cup grated Parmesan cheese
1 can (14 1/2 ounces) whole tomatoes, drained
Dressing:
2 to 2 1/2 tablespoons red wine vinegar
1 teaspoon minced garlic
1/2 teaspoon dried basil leaves
1/2 teaspoon dried oregano leaves
1/2 teaspoon dried parsley flakes
1/2 teaspoon salt
1/2 teaspoon coarse black pepper

1. Cook rotini as directed on package; rinse and drain. Mix rotini, artichoke hearts, black olives, onion, red pepper, and Parmesan cheese in large glass or plastic bowl.
2. Chop tomatoes and drain. Place tomatoes in single layer between double layer of paper towels. Press to remove juice. Stir tomatoes into rotini mixture.
3. Mix all dressing ingredients. Toss dressing and rotini mixture until evenly coated. Cover and refrigerate 1 hour to blend flavors.

OLD-FASHIONED MACARONI SALAD   4 servings

1 cup uncooked elbow macaroni (3 1/2 ounces)
1/3 cup chopped onion
1/3 cup chopped pimiento-stuffed green olives
1/3 cup chopped celery
1/4 cup diced carrot
Dressing:
1/4 cup low-fat yogurt
3 tablespoons salad dressing or mayonnaise
1 tablespoon white vinegar
1 teaspoon Dijon mustard
1/4 teaspoon salt
1/4 teaspoon coarse black pepper

1. Cook macaroni as directed on package; rinse and drain. Mix macaroni, onion, green olives, celery, and carrot in large glass or plastic bowl.
2. Mix all dressing ingredients. Toss dressing and macaroni mixture until evenly coated. Cover and refrigerate 1 hour to blend flavors. Serve with slotted spoon.

COLESLAW PASTA SALAD   4 servings

1 cup uncooked elbow macaroni (3 1/2 ounces)
1 1/2 cups Colorful Coleslaw (page 128), drained
   with dressing reserved
3/4 cup reserved dressing
1/4 teaspoon salt
1/4 teaspoon coarse black pepper

1. Cook macaroni as directed on package; rinse and drain.
2. Mix macaroni, coleslaw, 3/4 cup reserved dressing, salt, and pepper in large glass or plastic bowl until evenly coated. Serve immediately or cover and refrigerate until ready to serve.

OLD-FASHIONED POTATO SALAD   4 servings

2 1/2 cups hot cooked potato cubes (3 medium boiling potatoes)
1/3 cup chopped celery
1/3 cup chopped onion
1/3 cup chopped pimiento-stuffed green olives
Dressing:
1/4 cup low-fat yogurt
2 tablespoons salad dressing or mayonnaise
1 tablespoon white vinegar
1 teaspoon prepared mustard
1/2 teaspoon salt
1/2 teaspoon coarse black pepper

1. Mix potatoes, celery, onion, and green olives in large glass or plastic bowl.
2. Mix all dressing ingredients. Toss dressing and potato mixture until evenly coated. Cover and refrigerate 1 hour to blend flavors or until ready to serve. Serve with slotted spoon, if desired.

MEXICAN BEAN-POTATO SALAD   4 servings

3 cups hot cooked potato cubes (3 to 4 medium boiling potatoes)
1 can (15 ounces) red kidney beans, rinsed and drained
3/4 cup halved black olives
2/3 cup chopped green onions
1/2 cup chopped onion
Dressing:
2/3 cup salsa
2 tablespoons salad dressing or mayonnaise
2 teaspoons white vinegar
3/4 teaspoon salt
1/2 teaspoon coarse black pepper

1. Mix potatoes, kidney beans, black olives, green onions, and onion in large glass or plastic bowl.
2. Mix all dressing ingredients. Toss dressing and potato mixture until evenly coated. Cover and refrigerate 1 hour to blend flavors or until ready to serve.

BACON AND POTATO SALAD   4 servings

4 1/2 cups hot cooked potato cubes (4 to 5 medium boiling potatoes)
4 slices bacon, crisply cooked and crumbled (reserve 1 tablespoon
   bacon fat for dressing)
2/3 cup chopped green onions
1/2 cup chopped onion
1 large clove garlic, minced
Dressing:
3 tablespoons cider vinegar
2 tablespoons salad dressing or mayonnaise
1 tablespoon bacon fat
1 tablespoon vegetable oil
1/2 teaspoon salt
1/2 teaspoon coarse black pepper

1. Mix potatoes, bacon, green onions, onion, and garlic in large glass or
plastic bowl.
2. Mix all dressing ingredients. Toss dressing and potato mixture until
evenly coated. Serve warm.

ITALIAN-STYLE RICE SALAD   2 servings

1 1/2 cups hot cooked white rice
1 can (4 ounces) mushroom stems and pieces, drained
1/2 cup grated Parmesan cheese
1/3 cup chopped onion
1/4 cup salad dressing or mayonnaise
1 tablespoon lemon juice
1/2 teaspoon salt
1/4 teaspoon coarse black pepper
1 medium clove garlic, minced

Mix all ingredients in medium glass or plastic bowl. Serve immediately or
cover and refrigerate until chilled, if desired.

TOMATO-GREEN PEPPER SALAD   2 servings

10 to 12 cherry tomatoes, cut into fourths (1 cup)
1/4 cup chopped onion
1/4 cup chopped green bell pepper
3/4 teaspoon minced garlic
Dressing:
1 tablespoon red wine vinegar
1 tablespoon vegetable oil
2 teaspoons sugar
1/4 teaspoon salt
1/4 teaspoon coarse black pepper

1. Mix tomatoes, onion, green pepper, and garlic in small glass or plastic bowl.
2. Shake all dressing ingredients in tightly covered container. Toss dressing and tomato mixture until evenly coated. Cover and refrigerate 30 minutes to blend flavors or until ready to serve. Serve on salad greens, if desired.

ITALIAN-STYLE SALSA   2 cups

15 to 17 cherry tomatoes, cut into fourths (1 1/2 cups)
1/3 cup finely chopped fresh basil leaves
1/4 cup chopped black olives
1/4 cup chopped onion
1 tablespoon olive oil
1 tablespoon balsamic vinegar, scant
1/2 teaspoon minced garlic
1/8 teaspoon salt
1/8 teaspoon coarse black pepper

Mix all ingredients in medium glass or plastic bowl. Serve with grilled meats or on salad greens.

BOURBON BAKED BEANS   4 servings

1 can (16 ounces) pork and beans (pour off any liquid that has risen to
    top of can, up to 1/4 cup)
1/2 cup chopped onion
2 tablespoons light brown sugar
2 tablespoons ketchup
1 tablespoon bourbon
1 tablespoon molasses
1 teaspoon prepared mustard
1/4 teaspoon coarse black pepper
1/8 teaspoon garlic salt
Garnish: 2 slices bacon, crisply cooked and crumbled

Mix all ingredients in medium saucepan. Heat to boiling; reduce heat to low.
Simmer uncovered 5 to 7 minutes, stirring occasionally. Place in serving
bowl; sprinkle with crumbled bacon.

FRIJOLES PICANTE   4 servings

1 can (16 ounces) refried beans
2 tablespoons picante sauce
2 tablespoons canned chopped green chiles
1 large clove garlic, minced

Mix all ingredients in medium saucepan. Heat until boiling, stirring
frequently; reduce heat to low. Simmer uncovered 3 to 5 minutes, stirring
frequently.
NOTE: Heat in microwave, if preferred. Mix all ingredients in microwavable
bowl. Cover loosely with plastic wrap; heat in microwave on High (100%)
until heated through.

MEXICAN REFRIED BEAN TOAST   4 servings

French bread, cut into 1/2-inch slices
1 can (16 ounces) refried beans
4 to 5 teaspoons dry taco seasoning mix
Garnish: Shredded mozzarella or Monterey Jack cheese

1. Heat oven to 375°. Line a baking sheet with aluminum foil. Place bread slices on baking sheet in single layer. Bake bread 5 to 10 minutes, turning once, until crisp.
2. While bread slices are baking, mix refried beans and taco seasoning mix in microwavable bowl. Cover loosely with plastic wrap; heat in microwave on High (100%) until heated through.
3. Set oven control to broil. Spread desired amount of refried bean mixture over bread; sprinkle with cheese. Broil until cheese is melted.

MEXICAN REFRIED BEANS: Omit French bread and shredded cheese. Stir in 2 tablespoons salsa with the taco seasoning mix. Heat and serve as a side dish.

BROCCOLI-CAULIFLOWER GRATIN   4 servings

2 cups cauliflower florets
2 cups broccoli florets
2 tablespoons butter, cut into pieces
Salt and pepper
1/3 cup soft bread crumbs
1/4 cup grated Parmesan cheese

1. Heat about 1 inch water to boiling in medium saucepan; add cauliflower. Cover and boil 1 minute. Stir in broccoli; cover and boil 2 minutes. Drain.
2. Set oven control to broil. Spray an 11x7x2-inch baking pan with nonstick cooking spray. Place broccoli and cauliflower in baking pan. Toss broccoli mixture and butter until evenly coated. Sprinkle with salt and pepper.
3. Mix bread crumbs and Parmesan cheese. Sprinkle over vegetables. Broil until light brown.

SOUTHWESTERN CORN-ON-THE-COBB

4 servings

4 cooked fresh corn ears (boiled or grilled)
Southwestern Butter (below)

Serve hot corn ears with Southwestern Butter.

SOUTHWESTERN BUTTER

1/4 cup

Beat 1/4 cup butter, softened, with one of the following:
MEXICAN: 1/2 teaspoon chili powder and 1/2 teaspoon ground cumin
PICANTE: 1/4 cup picante sauce. Chill until firm.
TACO: 1 teaspoon dry taco seasoning mix

BLUE CHEESE BUTTER

1/3 cup

1/4 cup butter, softened
2 tablespoons crumbled blue cheese (1/2 ounce)
1/2 teaspoon dried chives

Beat butter, blue cheese, and chives. Serve immediately or cover and refrigerate until firm. Serve on baked potatoes, grilled steak, or toasted French bread.

PORTOBELLO MUSHROOM SAUTÉ

2 servings

1 tablespoon olive oil
2 portobello mushrooms, stems removed
1 tablespoon balsamic vinegar
1/2 teaspoon dried basil leaves
1/4 teaspoon salt
1/4 teaspoon coarse black pepper
1 tablespoon butter
Serve with: Toasted French bread

1. Heat oil in large skillet over medium heat. Add mushrooms to skillet. Sprinkle with balsamic vinegar, basil, salt, and pepper. Reduce heat to low; cook 5 minutes, turning once.
2. Add butter. Heat until butter is melted, stirring occasionally. Spoon sauce onto French bread; top with mushroom.

MUSHROOMS AND ONIONS   4 servings

1 tablespoon olive oil
1 medium onion, thinly sliced and separated into rings
8 ounces mushrooms, sliced
2 teaspoons soy sauce
1 teaspoon minced garlic
1/2 teaspoon dried thyme leaves
1/4 teaspoon salt
1/4 teaspoon coarse black pepper

1. Heat oil in large skillet over medium heat. Cook onion rings and mushrooms in oil 5 minutes, stirring frequently.
2. Stir in remaining ingredients. Reduce heat to low. Simmer uncovered about 1 minute to reduce sauce. Serve hot or cold.

CARAMELIZED ONIONS   2 servings

1 tablespoon margarine
1 large onion, thinly sliced and separated into rings
2 tablespoons honey
1/4 teaspoon salt
1/4 teaspoon dry mustard
1/8 teaspoon coarse black pepper

1. Melt margarine in large skillet over medium heat. Cook onion rings in margarine 6 minutes, stirring frequently.
2. Stir in remaining ingredients; reduce heat to low. Simmer about 2 minutes, stirring frequently, until onion rings are golden brown.

HERBED SPAGHETTI   2 servings

2 tablespoons butter
2 tablespoons olive oil
2 cups hot cooked spaghetti
1 teaspoon dried parsley flakes
1/2 teaspoon chicken bouillon granules
1/4 teaspoon dried basil leaves
1/4 teaspoon dried oregano leaves
1/4 teaspoon coarse black pepper
1/4 cup grated Parmesan cheese

Melt butter with olive oil in large saucepan over medium heat. Stir in cooked spaghetti, parsley, chicken bouillon granules, basil, oregano, and pepper, tossing to coat. Heat over medium heat until heated through. Quickly stir in Parmesan cheese, tossing to coat. Immediately place spaghetti on serving plates.

TOMATO-ARTICHOKE   2 servings
SPAGHETTI SAUCE

1 can (14 1/2 ounces) whole tomatoes, drained
1 can (8 ounces) tomato sauce
3/4 cup chopped canned artichoke hearts, well drained
1/2 cup halved black olives
1/4 cup vegetable oil
1 teaspoon minced garlic
1 teaspoon dried basil leaves
1 teaspoon dried parsley flakes
1/4 teaspoon salt
1/4 teaspoon coarse black pepper
Serve with: Spaghetti

Coarsely chop tomatoes and drain. Mix tomatoes and remaining ingredients in large saucepan. Heat to boiling; reduce heat to low. Simmer uncovered 15 minutes, stirring occasionally. Serve over spaghetti.

PARMESAN SPAGHETTI WITH BLACK OLIVES

2 servings

2 tablespoons butter
2 cups hot cooked spaghetti
1/4 teaspoon salt
1/4 teaspoon coarse black pepper
1/3 cup grated Parmesan cheese
1/2 cup halved black olives, room temperature

1. Melt butter in large saucepan over medium heat. Stir in cooked spaghetti, salt, and pepper; cook until heated through. Quickly stir in Parmesan cheese, tossing until spaghetti is evenly coated.
2. Immediately place spaghetti in serving bowl. Sprinkle with black olives.

CREAMY PESTO SAUCE

about 1 2/3 cups

1 cup White Sauce (page 117 or prepared white sauce)
1/2 cup Pesto (below or prepared pesto)
1/3 cup grated Parmesan cheese
Serve with: Hot cooked pasta

Mix all ingredients in small saucepan. Heat over medium heat, stirring occasionally, until cheese is melted and mixture is smooth. Toss sauce and hot pasta.

PESTO

about 1/2 cup

1 cup firmly packed fresh basil leaves
6 tablespoons grated Parmesan cheese
3 tablespoons olive oil
2 tablespoons chopped walnuts
1 tablespoon water
1 teaspoon dried dill weed
1 teaspoon dried parsley flakes
1/2 teaspoon minced garlic
1/8 teaspoon salt
1/8 teaspoon coarse black pepper

Place all ingredients in food processor. Cover and blend, stopping occasionally to scrape down sides, until smooth.

POLENTA   4 to 6 servings

2 1/4 cups chicken broth
1 cup yellow cornmeal
1 cup cold water
1/2 teaspoon salt
Garnish: Grated Parmesan cheese

1. Heat chicken broth to boiling in large saucepan. Mix cornmeal, cold water, and salt. Gradually add cornmeal mixture to chicken broth. Cook, stirring constantly, until mixture boils; reduce heat to low.
2. Simmer 10 minutes, stirring constantly, until mixture is very thick. Place in serving dish. Sprinkle with Parmesan cheese.

BAKED POLENTA: Spray a 9-inch pie plate with nonstick cooking spray. Spread cooked polenta in plate. Press plastic wrap onto surface to smooth and to cover; refrigerate 30 minutes or until firm. Heat oven to 375°. Remove plastic wrap and sprinkle with Parmesan cheese. Bake uncovered 25 minutes or until heated through. Let stand 5 minutes before cutting.

POMMES ANNA   2 servings

Butter-flavored nonstick cooking spray
2 medium potatoes, peeled and thinly sliced
Salt and pepper

1. Heat oven to 425°. Line a 9-inch pie plate with aluminum foil and spray with butter-flavored nonstick cooking spray.
2. Arrange a layer of overlapping potato slices in pie plate. Spray generously with butter-flavored nonstick cooking spray; sprinkle with salt and pepper. Continue adding 2 more layers of potatoes, spraying with butter-flavored nonstick cooking spray and sprinkling with salt and pepper.
3. Spray an approximate 12-inch square of aluminum foil with butter-flavored nonstick cooking spray. Place sprayed side down on potatoes; tightly seal edges. Press firmly to compact the potatoes.
4. Bake 30 minutes. Remove aluminum foil and bake 30 minutes longer. Invert the potatoes onto a heat-proof plate and cut into wedges to serve.

OVEN-FRIED POTATOES   2 servings

2 medium unpeeled potatoes, cut lengthwise into 1/2-inch strips
1 tablespoon vegetable oil
3/4 teaspoon minced garlic
1/4 to 1/2 teaspoon salt
1/8 teaspoon coarse black pepper

1. Heat oven to 400°. Line a shallow baking pan with aluminum foil and spray with nonstick cooking spray.
2. Place potato strips in single layer between double layer of paper towels to remove excess moisture. Place potatoes in pan; toss with oil. Sprinkle with garlic, salt, and pepper.
3. Bake uncovered 30 minutes.

BASIL OVEN-FRIED POTATOES: After baking potatoes, sprinkle with 1/2 to 3/4 teaspoon dried basil leaves.

BLACK OLIVE OVEN-FRIED POTATOES: Substitute 1 tablespoon olive oil for vegetable oil. After baking 25 minutes, sprinkle with 1/4 cup chopped black olives. Bake 5 minutes longer.

CAJUN OVEN-FRIED POTATOES: Reduce salt to 1/4 teaspoon. In additional to garlic and pepper, sprinkle with 1 tablespoon Cajun seasoning.

CHILI-FLAVORED OVEN-FRIED POTATOES: Omit garlic. In addition to salt and pepper, sprinkle with 1 teaspoon chili powder, 1/4 teaspoon dried oregano leaves, and 1/8 teaspoon ground cumin.

ONION-FLAVORED OVEN-FRIED POTATOES: Omit garlic, salt, and pepper. After tossing with oil, sprinkle with 2 tablespoons dry onion soup mix.

ROSEMARY OVEN-FRIED POTATOES: After baking potatoes, sprinkle with 1/2 to 3/4 teaspoon dried rosemary leaves.

TARRAGON OVEN-FRIED POTATOES: After baking potatoes, sprinkle with 1/2 to 3/4 teaspoon dried tarragon leaves.

THYME OVEN-FRIED POTATOES: After baking potatoes, sprinkle with 1/2 to 3/4 teaspoon dried thyme leaves.

CREAMY STUFFED POTATOES   2 servings

2 medium potatoes
1/2 cup sour cream or low-fat yogurt, drained
2 tablespoons grated Parmesan cheese
1/8 teaspoon salt
1/8 teaspoon coarse black pepper
2 tablespoons minced green onion
Garnish: Chopped green onion and paprika

1. Cook potatoes in oven or microwave until tender.
2. Heat oven to 350°. Line a baking sheet with aluminum foil.
3. Cut potatoes lengthwise in half; scoop out inside, leaving a thin shell. Mash potatoes with sour cream, Parmesan cheese, salt, and pepper until no lumps remain. Stir in green onion. Fill potato shells with potato mixture. Place on baking sheet.
4. Bake uncovered 10 to 15 minutes or until hot. Sprinkle with green onion and paprika.

PARMESAN-TOPPED POTATOES   2 servings

2 medium potatoes
Salt and pepper
1/4 cup sour cream
2 tablespoons grated Parmesan cheese

1. Cook potatoes in oven or microwave until tender.
2. Set oven control to broil. Line a baking sheet with aluminum foil.
3. Cut potatoes lengthwise in half. Place potato halves, cut side up, on baking sheet. Sprinkle cut side of potatoes with salt and pepper.
4. Mix sour cream and parmesan cheese. Spread sour cream mixture over cut side of potatoes. Broil until bubbly and Parmesan cheese is light brown.

CREAMY MASHED POTATOES   4 servings

2 cups hot mashed potatoes
2/3 cup low-fat cottage cheese
Salt and pepper

Beat mashed potatoes and cottage cheese in medium bowl with electric mixer on high speed until very smooth. Stir in salt and pepper.

MEXICAN MASHED POTATOES   4 servings

3 cups hot cooked potato cubes (3 to 4 medium potatoes)
1 can (8 3/4 ounces) whole kernel corn, drained with liquid
   reserved
3 tablespoons reserved corn liquid
2 to 4 tablespoons milk
2 tablespoons butter, cut into pieces
1/3 cup chopped green onions
1 jar (2 ounces) chopped pimientos, drained (1/4 cup)
1/2 teaspoon salt

Mash potatoes with 3 tablespoons corn liquid, 2 tablespoons milk, and butter until no lumps remain in large saucepan over low heat. Beat in additional milk to thin (up to 2 tablespoons), if necessary. Stir in corn, green onions, pimientos, and salt. Cook until hot, stirring occasionally.

GARLIC MASHED POTATOES   4 servings

3 1/2 cups hot cooked potato cubes (3 to 4 medium potatoes)
3/4 cup milk, divided
2 1/2 teaspoons chicken bouillon granules
1/2 teaspoon minced garlic
Salt

Mash potatoes with 1/2 cup milk, chicken bouillon granules, and garlic until no lumps remain in medium saucepan over low heat. Beat in remaining 1/4 cup milk and salt. Cook about 1 minute, stirring frequently, until hot.

BASIL-GARLIC MASHED POTATOES: Prepare Garlic Mashed Potatoes. Stir in 1/4 cup chopped fresh basil leaves.

ITALIAN-STYLE SCALLOPED POTATOES AND TOMATOES

4 servings

3 medium potatoes, peeled and thinly sliced
Salt and coarse black pepper
1 can (14 1/2 ounces) whole tomatoes
1/4 cup vegetable oil
1 large clove garlic, minced
1 teaspoon dried basil leaves
1 teaspoon dried oregano leaves
1 teaspoon sugar
1/4 teaspoon salt

1. Heat oven to 375°. Line an 11x7x2-inch baking dish with aluminum foil and spray with nonstick cooking spray.
2. Place half of potato slices in dish. Sprinkle with salt and pepper.
3. Coarsely chop tomatoes, reserving juice. Mix tomatoes, tomato juice, oil, garlic, basil, oregano, sugar, and salt. Spread half of tomato mixture over potato slices. Top with remaining potato slices. Sprinkle with salt and pepper. Spread remaining tomato mixture over potato slices.
4. Bake uncovered 50 to 60 minutes.

OVEN-FRIED POTATO AND SWEET POTATO

2 servings

1 medium unpeeled potato, cut lengthwise into 1/2-inch strips
1 medium unpeeled sweet potato, cut lengthwise into 1/2-inch strips
2 teaspoons vegetable oil
1 large clove garlic, minced
Salt and pepper
Garnish: Dried parsley flakes

1. Heat oven to 400°. Line a shallow baking pan with aluminum foil and spray with nonstick cooking spray.
2. Place potatoes in pan; toss with oil. Sprinkle with garlic, salt, and pepper.
3. Bake uncovered 30 minutes. Sprinkle with parsley.

STIR-FRIED SWEET POTATOES   2 servings

1 tablespoon vegetable oil
2 medium sweet potatoes, cut lengthwise into 1/4-inch strips
Salt

Heat oil in large skillet over medium heat. Cook sweet potatoes in oil 5 to 8 minutes or until crisp-tender, stirring constantly. Sprinkle with salt.

SANTA FE RICE   4 servings

2 1/2 cups water
2 chicken bouillon cubes
1 beef bouillon cube
1 cup uncooked regular long grain rice

1. Heat water, chicken bouillon cubes, and beef bouillon cube to boiling in medium saucepan, stirring occasionally to dissolve cubes. Stir in rice. Heat to boiling; reduce heat to low. Cover and simmer 20 minutes.
2. Turn off heat. Let stand covered 5 minutes.

RICE AND VERMICELLI   4 servings

Butter-flavored nonstick cooking spray
1/2 cup broken pieces of vermicelli or spaghetti
2 1/2 cups chicken bouillon
1 cup uncooked regular long grain rice
1/8 teaspoon garlic powder
1/8 teaspoon coarse black pepper

1. Heat butter-flavored nonstick cooking spray in large skillet over medium heat. Add vermicelli. Stir-fry on medium heat until brown.
2. Heat bouillon to boiling in medium saucepan. Stir in vermicelli, rice, garlic powder, and pepper. Heat to boiling; reduce heat to low. Cover and simmer 20 minutes.
3. Turn off heat. Let stand covered 5 minutes.

RICE AND BLACK BEANS   4 servings

1 1/2 cups chicken bouillon
1/2 cup uncooked regular long grain rice
1/2 cup chopped onion
1 teaspoon minced garlic
1/4 teaspoon dried oregano leaves
1/4 teaspoon coarse black pepper
1 cup black beans, rinsed and drained
Salt

1. Heat chicken bouillon to boiling in medium saucepan. Stir in rice, onion, garlic, oregano, and pepper. Heat to boiling; reduce heat to low. Cover and simmer 20 minutes.
2. Turn off heat. Stir in black beans. Add salt, if desired. Cover and let stand 5 minutes.

CAJUN PILAF   4 servings

1/2 cup chopped smoked sausage links (about 2 1/2 ounces)
1 teaspoon vegetable oil
1/2 cup chopped onion
1/2 cup chopped green bell pepper
1 can (14 1/2 ounces) whole tomatoes
1 cup water
1 teaspoon minced garlic
1/4 teaspoon dried thyme leaves
1/4 teaspoon coarse black pepper
1/8 to 1/4 teaspoon salt
2/3 cup uncooked regular long grain rice, heaping
1/2 cup chopped green onions

1. Fry sausage in medium skillet until brown. Remove to paper towel to drain. Add oil to skillet; heat over medium-high heat. Cook onion and pepper in oil until crisp-tender, stirring occasionally.
2. Coarsely chop tomatoes, reserving juice. Mix tomatoes, tomato juice, sausage, onion mixture, water, garlic, thyme, pepper, and salt in large saucepan. Heat to boiling; stir in rice. Reduce heat to low. Cover and simmer 20 minutes, stirring occasionally.
3. Turn off heat. Stir in green onions. Cover and let stand 5 minutes.

RICE AND RED BEANS   4 servings

1 can (15 ounces) red kidney beans, drained with liquid reserved
1/2 cup reserved kidney bean liquid
1 cup beef bouillon
1/2 cup uncooked regular long grain rice
1/2 cup chopped onion
1/4 cup chopped celery
1 teaspoon minced garlic
1 teaspoon dried parsley flakes
1/4 teaspoon dried thyme leaves
1/4 teaspoon coarse black pepper
1/4 teaspoon salt
1/8 teaspoon garlic powder

1. Drain kidney beans, reserving 1/2 cup kidney bean liquid. Set aside kidney beans.
2. Heat 1/2 cup kidney bean liquid and beef bouillon to boiling in medium saucepan. Stir in rice, onion, celery, and garlic. Heat to boiling; reduce heat to low. Cover and simmer 15 minutes.
3. Stir in kidney beans, parsley, thyme, pepper, salt, and garlic powder. Cover and simmer 5 minutes.
4. Turn off heat. Let stand covered 5 minutes.

MUSHROOM RISOTTO   4 servings

1 1/4 cups chicken broth
1 can (4 ounces) sliced mushrooms, drained with liquid reserved
1/3 cup reserved mushroom liquid
2/3 cup uncooked regular long grain rice, heaping
1 medium clove garlic, minced
1/4 teaspoon salt
1/8 teaspoon coarse black pepper
3 tablespoons grated Parmesan cheese

1. Heat chicken broth and 1/3 cup mushroom liquid to boiling in medium saucepan. Stir in mushrooms, rice, garlic, salt, and pepper. Heat to boiling; reduce heat to low. Cover and simmer 20 minutes.
2. Turn off heat. Let stand covered 5 minutes. Stir in Parmesan cheese. Serve immediately.

ITALIAN-STYLE RICE AND VEGETABLES

4 servings

1 1/2 cups chicken bouillon
1/2 cup uncooked regular long grain rice
1/2 cup chopped onion
1 teaspoon minced garlic
2/3 cup chopped zucchini
1/2 cup chopped red bell pepper
1/2 cup halved black olives
1/2 cup grated Parmesan cheese

1. Heat chicken bouillon to boiling in medium saucepan. Stir in rice, onion, and garlic. Heat to boiling; reduce heat to low. Cover and simmer 15 minutes.
2. Stir in zucchini. Cover and simmer 5 minutes. Turn off heat. Stir in red pepper and black olives. Cover and let stand 5 minutes. Stir in Parmesan cheese. Serve immediately.

PESTO RICE

2 servings

1 1/3 cups water
1/2 cup uncooked regular long grain rice
1/2 cup pesto
1/4 teaspoon salt
1/4 teaspoon coarse black pepper

1. Heat water to boiling in medium saucepan. Stir in rice. Reduce heat to low; cover and simmer 20 minutes.
2. Turn off heat. Stir in pesto, salt, and pepper. Cover and let stand 5 minutes.

CHICKEN-FLAVORED RICE

Prepare uncooked regular long grain rice or instant rice according to package directions, substituting chicken bouillon for water.

BEEF-FLAVORED RICE: Substitute beef bouillon for chicken bouillon.

ONION-FRIED RICE   3 to 4 servings

1 tablespoon vegetable oil
1/2 cup chopped green onions
1/2 cup chopped onion
1 1/2 cups cold cooked rice
1 egg
1 tablespoon water
1 tablespoon dry sherry
1 tablespoon soy sauce
Coarse black pepper

1. Heat oil in large skillet over medium-high heat. Cook green onions and onion in oil until crisp-tender, stirring constantly. Stir in rice; cook until heated through, stirring frequently.
2. Beat egg and water with fork until uniform yellow. Push rice mixture to side of skillet. Spray other side of skillet with nonstick cooking spray. Pour egg mixture into skillet over nonstick cooking spray; cook over medium heat until egg mixture thickens. Stir egg mixture into rice mixture. Stir in sherry, soy sauce, and pepper.

PEPPER-FRIED RICE: Substitute 1/2 cup chopped red bell pepper and 1/2 cup chopped green bell pepper for green onions and onion.

MANDARIN SNOW PEAS   4 servings

1 package (8 ounces) frozen snow peas, thawed
1 can (11 ounces) Mandarin oranges, drained
1 tablespoon butter
Salt and pepper

1. Heat 1 inch water to boiling in medium saucepan. Add snow peas and reduce heat to medium. Cover and simmer 2 minutes or until crisp-tender. Drain.
2. Gently stir in Mandarin oranges, butter, salt, and pepper. Heat until butter is melted and oranges are heated through.

SOUTHWESTERN SUCCOTASH   4 servings

1 tablespoon vegetable oil
2 cups cubed zucchini (2 to 3 medium zucchini)
1/2 cup chopped onion
1 large clove garlic, minced
1 can (8 3/4 ounces) whole kernel corn, drained (1 cup)
1/4 teaspoon salt
1/4 teaspoon coarse black pepper
Garnish: 1/2 cup shredded Cheddar cheese (2 ounces)

1. Heat oil in large skillet over medium-high heat. Cook zucchini in oil 2 minutes, stirring constantly. Stir in onion and garlic; cook 1 minute or until onion is crisp-tender, stirring constantly. Stir in corn, salt, and pepper. Cook 1 to 2 minutes, stirring occasionally, until hot.
2. Set oven control to broil. Spray an 11x7x2-inch baking pan with nonstick cooking spray. Place zucchini mixture in pan. Sprinkle with cheese. Broil until cheese is melted.

SQUASH-TOMATO MEDLEY   4 servings

2 teaspoons vegetable oil
1 1/2 cups cubed zucchini (1 to 2 medium zucchini)
1 1/2 cups cubed crookneck squash (1 to 2 medium crookneck squash)
1 teaspoon minced garlic
1 can (14 1/2 ounces) whole tomatoes, drained
1/4 teaspoon salt
1/4 teaspoon coarse black pepper

1. Heat oil in large skillet over medium-high heat. Cook zucchini, crookneck squash, and garlic in oil 2 minutes, stirring frequently.
2. Coarsely chop tomatoes and drain. Stir in tomatoes, salt, and pepper. Cook until heated through, stirring occasionally.

ITALIAN SQUASH COMBO   4 servings

2 teaspoons vegetable oil
1 1/2 cups sliced zucchini (1 to 2 medium zucchini)
1 1/2 cups sliced crookneck squash (1 to 2 medium crookneck squash)
1 teaspoon minced garlic
1 medium red bell pepper, cut into 1/4-inch strips
2 to 3 tablespoons grated Parmesan cheese
1/2 teaspoon dried basil leaves
1/2 teaspoon dried thyme leaves
1/4 teaspoon salt
1/4 teaspoon coarse black pepper

1. Heat oil in large skillet over medium-high heat. Cook zucchini, crookneck squash, and garlic in oil until squash are light brown on all sides. Stir in red pepper. Cook until red pepper is crisp-tender, stirring constantly.
2. Stir in remaining ingredients. Serve immediately.

STIR-FRIED ITALIAN VEGETABLES

4 servings

2 tablespoons olive oil
1 medium potato, cut into 1-inch pieces
1 medium zucchini, cut into 1-inch slices
1 medium red bell pepper, coarsely chopped
1 medium onion, cut into eighths
8 ounces whole mushrooms
2 teaspoons minced garlic
1 teaspoon dried thyme leaves
1 teaspoon dried basil leaves
1/4 teaspoon salt
1/4 teaspoon coarse black pepper

Heat oil over medium-high heat in large skillet. Cook potatoes in oil 3 minutes, stirring constantly. Reduce heat to medium; stir in zucchini. Cook 1 minute, stirring constantly. Stir in red pepper, onion, mushrooms, and garlic. Cook 8 minutes or until vegetables are crisp-tender, stirring constantly. Stir in thyme, basil, salt, and pepper.

6
DESSERTS

Do you have a sweet tooth? If you answered yes, satisfy your cravings with the easy-to-prepare desserts included in this chapter. Although all of the recipes are simple, some take longer to make than the other recipes in this cookbook. Because I like to relax when I'm camping, I prefer quick-and-easy dishes for most meals. However, baking desserts is an activity in which I take great pleasure. If you share my passion, you will enjoy trying all of the delicious dessert recipes.

CHOCOLATE PEANUT BUTTER   about 2/3 cup

3/4 cup milk chocolate chips or semisweet chocolate chips
1/3 cup creamy peanut butter

1. Place chocolate chips in microwavable bowl. Heat in microwave on High (100%), stopping and stirring, until melted and smooth. Stir in peanut butter.
2. Spread mixture over cookies or crackers. If thicker spread is desired, cover and refrigerate 30 to 45 minutes.

CHOCOLATE VELVET   about 1 cup

1 1/2 cups milk chocolate chips or semisweet chocolate chips
1/2 cup half-and-half
Serve with: Ice cream or frozen yogurt

Place chips and half-and-half in medium microwavable bowl. Heat in microwave on High (100%), stopping and stirring, until melted and smooth. Serve warm over ice cream. Refrigerate any remaining sauce.

CANDY BAR SAUCE   about 1 3/4 cups

1/2 cup semisweet chocolate chips
1/2 cup butterscotch chips
1 can (14 ounces) sweetened condensed milk
2 tablespoons margarine, cut into pieces

Place chocolate chips, butterscotch chips, and sweetened condensed milk in large microwavable bowl. Heat in microwave on High (100%), stopping and stirring, until smooth. Add margarine; stir until margarine is melted and mixture is smooth. Serve warm over ice cream. Refrigerate any remaining sauce.

DESSERT NACHOS   4 servings

4 flour tortillas (6 inches in diameter)
Butter-flavored nonstick cooking spray
2 tablespoons sugar
1/2 teaspoon ground cinnamon
2 tablespoons semisweet chocolate chips
2 tablespoons butterscotch chips

1. Heat oven to 400°. Line a shallow baking pan with aluminum foil.
2. Stack tortillas and cut into fourths. Place tortilla wedges in pan; spray with butter-flavored nonstick cooking spray. Mix sugar and cinnamon; sprinkle over tortilla wedges.
3. Bake 8 to 10 minutes or until crisp. Remove tortilla wedges from pan. Cool on wire rack.
4. Line a 12-inch pizza pan with aluminum foil. Place tortilla wedges in single layer in pan.
5. Place chocolate chips and butterscotch chips in microwavable bowl. Heat in microwave on High (100%), stopping and stirring, until smooth. Place mixture in a reclosable plastic bag. Snip a bottom corner of bag; pipe mixture over tortilla wedges.

FRAPPUCCINO   1 serving (about 8 ounces)

1 cup frozen chocolate yogurt
2 tablespoons hot milk
1 teaspoon instant coffee granules

2 to 3 teaspoons sugar
1/8 teaspoon ground cinnamon

1. Place frozen yogurt in blender.
2. Mix hot milk and instant coffee granules, stirring until granules are dissolved. Pour coffee mixture over frozen yogurt. Add sugar and cinnamon to blender. Cover and process, using short on and off pulses, until smooth. Pour into tall glass to serve.

MEXICAN SUNDAE

Chocolate or Coffee ice cream
Candy Bar Sauce (page 156)
Dessert Nachos (page 156--omit Step #4 and Step #5)

Place ice cream in serving dish. Spoon Candy Bar Sauce over ice cream. Garnish rim of dish with Dessert Nachos.

CRISPY CANDY   25 pieces candy

Butter-flavored nonstick cooking spray
1 3/4 cups semisweet chocolate chips, milk chocolate chips, or cinnamon
   chips
3 tablespoons margarine, cut into pieces
1 1/2 cups crisp rice cereal

1. Line an 8-inch square pan with aluminum foil. Spray with butter-flavored nonstick cooking spray.
2. Place chips and margarine in microwavable bowl. Heat chips and margarine in microwave on Medium-high (70%), stopping and stirring, 1/2 to 1 minute or until mostly melted. Stir in crisp rice cereal. Mixture is very thick. Turn mixture into pan. Smooth surface by firmly pressing with back of a spoon.
3. Refrigerate uncovered 25 to 30 minutes or until firm. Cut into squares with sharp knife. Cover and store at room temperature.

CRISPY PEANUT BUTTER CANDY: Substitute 1 3/4 cups peanut butter chips for above recommended chips and 3 tablespoons creamy peanut butter for margarine.

MAPLE-PECAN FUDGE   2 pounds

1 1/2 cups semisweet chocolate chips
1 1/2 cups milk chocolate chips
1 can (14 ounces) sweetened condensed milk
2 teaspoons imitation maple extract
1 cup chopped toasted pecans (page 26) or chopped pecans

1. Line a 9-inch square pan with aluminum foil; grease with butter.
2. Place chocolate chips and milk chocolate chips in microwavable bowl.
Heat in microwave on High (100%) 1 minute. Stir in sweetened condensed
milk. Heat on High (100%), stopping and stirring, until melted and smooth.
Stir in maple extract and pecans. Immediately pour into pan, spreading
evenly.
3. Cover and refrigerate about 2 hours or until firm. Cut into squares.

COOKIE PIZZETTES   8 servings

1 package (18 ounces) refrigerated sugar cookie dough
1 package (8 ounces) cream cheese, softened
1/2 cup powdered sugar
Desired fruit toppings: Sliced fresh fruit (strawberries, bananas,
    peaches, or kiwis), blueberries, raspberries, or cubed pineapple
Garnish: Chocolate-flavored syrup, room temperature

1. Heat oven to 350°.
2. Cut sugar cookie dough into 8 slices, each slice about 1 inch thick.
Roll each slice on a lightly floured surface into a 4 1/2-inch circle. Place 4
cookies on ungreased 13x9-inch baking sheet.
3. Bake 11 to 13 minutes or until light golden brown. Cool on baking
sheet 1 minute. Remove cookies from baking sheet. Cool on wire rack. Bake
remaining 4 cookies.
4. Mix cream cheese and powdered sugar; spread over cookies. Arrange
desired fruit toppings on cream cheese mixture. Drizzle with syrup.

MICROWAVE S'MORES 1 serving

2 graham crackers (honey, cinnamon, or chocolate)*
Milk chocolate candy bar
1 large marshmallow

1. Place 1 graham cracker on microwavable plate. Cut candy bar to fit cracker and place on cracker. Use remaining candy bar for another S'more. Cut marshmallow in half; place cut sides down on candy bar.
2. Heat in microwave on High (100%) 15 to 20 seconds or until marshmallow is softened. Top with remaining graham cracker, pressing to adhere. Cool 30 seconds. Serve.
*Substitute one of the following store-bought cookies for graham crackers, if desired:

Chocolate chip cookies
Gingersnaps
Pecan shortbread

Vanilla wafers
Sugar cookies
Peanut butter cookies

OVEN-BAKED S'MORES 6 servings

12 graham crackers
**6 tablespoons semisweet chocolate chips, milk chocolate chips,
    butterscotch chips, or peanut butter chips***
6 large marshmallows

1. Heat oven to 350°. Line a 13x9x2-inch baking pan with foil. Place 6 graham crackers in pan.
2. Place 1 tablespoon chocolate chips on each cracker. Cut marshmallows in half; place cut sides down on chips, pressing to adhere.
3. Bake 8 minutes or until marshmallows are puffed and light brown. Place remaining graham crackers on top of marshmallows, pressing to adhere. Bake 2 minutes longer. Cool 5 minutes in pan. Serve.
*Substitute an equivalent amount of one of the following ingredients for the chips, if desired:

Milk chocolate candy bar
Milk chocolate peanut butter cup
Peanut butter
Peanut butter and chocolate chips

Crisp rice candy bar
Nutella®
Peanut butter and sliced banana

CRANBERRY-WHITE CHOCOLATE CHIP COOKIES

3 1/2 dozen

1/2 cup margarine, melted
2/3 cup packed light brown sugar
1/2 cup sugar
1 egg
1 teaspoon orange extract
2 cups flour
1/2 teaspoon ground cinnamon
3/4 teaspoon baking soda
1/2 teaspoon salt
1 cup white baking chips
2/3 cup sweetened dried cranberries

1. Mix margarine, brown sugar, and sugar in large bowl. Beat in egg and orange extract. Stir in flour, cinnamon, baking soda, and salt. Stir in white baking chips and dried cranberries.
2. Heat oven to 350°. Shape dough into 1-inch balls; place about 2 inches apart on lightly greased baking sheet. Bake 10 to 12 minutes. Center of cookie will be soft and somewhat doughy. Remove cookies from baking sheet. Cool on paper towel.

GERMAN CHOCOLATE CHIP COOKIES

3 1/2 to 4 dozen

1/2 cup margarine, melted
1/2 cup sugar
1/2 cup packed light brown sugar
1 egg
1 teaspoon vanilla extract
1 3/4 cups flour
3 tablespoons unsweetened cocoa powder
1 teaspoon baking soda
1/2 teaspoon salt, scant
1 cup milk chocolate chips
1/2 cup flaked coconut
1/2 cup chopped pecans

1. Mix margarine, sugar, and brown sugar in large bowl. Beat in egg and vanilla. Stir in flour, cocoa, baking soda, and salt. Stir in milk chocolate chips, flaked coconut, and pecans. Cover and refrigerate 2 hours or until firm.

2. Heat oven to 350°. Shape dough into 1-inch balls; place about 2 inches apart on lightly greased baking sheet. Bake 7 to 9 minutes. Center of cookie will be soft and somewhat doughy. Remove cookies from baking sheet. Cool on paper towel.

MEXICAN CHOCOLATE CHIP COOKIES

3 to 3 1/2 dozen

1/2 cup margarine, melted
1/2 cup sugar
1/2 cup packed light brown sugar
1 egg
2 teaspoons instant espresso powder
1 tablespoon coffee-flavored liqueur
1 3/4 to 1 7/8 cups flour
1 teaspoon ground cinnamon
1 teaspoon baking soda
1/2 teaspoon salt, scant
1 cup semisweet chocolate chips
1/2 cup chopped pecans

1. Mix margarine, sugar, and brown sugar in large bowl. Beat in egg. Dissolve instant espresso powder in coffee-flavored liqueur. Stir in liqueur mixture. Stir in 1 3/4 cups flour, cinnamon, baking soda, and salt. If dough is too sticky, gradually stir in flour (up to 2 tablespoons) to make dough stiffer. Stir in chocolate chips and pecans. Cover and refrigerate 2 hours or until firm.

2. Heat oven to 350°. Shape dough into 1-inch balls; place about 2 inches apart on lightly greased baking sheet. Bake 9 to 10 minutes. Center of cookie will be soft and somewhat doughy. Remove cookies from baking sheet. Cool on paper towel.

AMERICA'S BEST BROWNIES   16 brownies

1 cup sugar
1/2 cup margarine, melted
5 tablespoons unsweetened cocoa powder
2 eggs
1 teaspoon vanilla extract
1/2 cup flour
1/4 teaspoon salt
1/2 cup chopped pecans or walnuts, if desired

1. Heat oven to 350°. Line an 8-inch square baking dish with aluminum foil.
Spray with nonstick cooking spray; lightly flour.
2. Mix sugar, margarine, and cocoa in large bowl. Beat in eggs and vanilla.
Stir in flour and salt. Stir in pecans, if desired. Spread in dish.
3. Bake 25 to 30 minutes or until toothpick inserted in center comes out
clean. Cool in dish on wire rack. Cut into squares.

BLACK WALNUT BROWNIES: Substitute 1 teaspoon imitation black
walnut extract for the vanilla and increase chopped walnuts to 3/4 cup.
After baking, immediately drizzle 1 tablespoon brandy over brownies.
CHERRY-ALMOND BROWNIES: Substitute 1 teaspoon almond
extract for the vanilla and 1/4 cup chopped almonds for 1/2 cup pecans
or walnuts. Stir in 1/2 cup chopped maraschino cherries, well drained,
with the almonds.
CHIPPETY BROWNIES: Increase flour to 3/4 cup. Omit nuts. Stir in
1/4 cup semisweet chocolate chips, 1/4 cup butterscotch chips, 1/4 cup milk
chocolate chips, and 1/4 cup peanut butter chips.
CHOCOLATE FRUITCAKE BROWNIES: Substitute
1 teaspoon imitation black walnut extract for the vanilla and add
1 tablespoon brandy. Stir in 1/2 cup mixed candied fruit, chopped, and
1/2 cup chopped dates with the walnuts. After baking, immediately
drizzle 1 tablespoon brandy over brownies.
CHOCOLATE-PEANUT BUTTER BROWNIES: Decrease
margarine to 1/4 cup, melted, and add 1/4 cup creamy peanut butter.
Omit nuts.

CHUNKY BROWNIES: Omit nuts; stir in 1 cup semisweet chocolate chunks. After spreading batter in dish, sprinkle with 1/2 cup white chocolate chunks, pressing slightly to embed. Bake 25 to 30 minutes or until brownies are firmly set.

COCONUT BROWNIES: Substitute 2 teaspoons imitation coconut extract for the vanilla and stir in 1 can (3 1/2 ounces) flaked coconut after beating in flour and salt. Omit nuts. Brownies are done when toothpick inserted in center comes out with only a moist crumb.

DATE-NUT BROWNIES: Increase walnuts to 3/4 cup. Stir in 3/4 cup chopped dates with the walnuts.

MAPLE-PECAN BROWNIES: Substitute 1 cup packed light or dark brown sugar for the sugar and substitute 1 teaspoon imitation maple extract for the vanilla. Increase chopped pecans to 3/4 cup.

MEXICAN BROWNIES: Substitute 1 tablespoon coffee-flavored liqueur for the vanilla and add 3/4 teaspoon ground cinnamon with the flour. Omit nuts. After baking and cooling, drizzle 2 tablespoons coffee-flavored liqueur over brownies. Let stand until liqueur is absorbed before cutting.

MOCHA BROWNIES: Decrease unsweetened cocoa powder to 3 tablespoons. Dissolve 1 tablespoon instant espresso powder in vanilla. Omit nuts.

RASPBERRY MARBLED BROWNIES: Omit nuts. Spread batter in dish. Drop 1/4 cup red raspberry preserves by teaspoonfuls evenly over batter, indenting slightly with spoon. Pull knife through batter and preserves for marbled design.

RUM-RAISIN BROWNIES: Substitute 1 tablespoon dark rum for the vanilla. Add 3/4 teaspoon ground cinnamon with the flour. Stir in 1/2 cup semisweet chocolate chips and 1/2 cup raisins with the nuts. After baking, immediately drizzle 2 tablespoons dark rum over brownies. Let stand until liquor is absorbed before cutting.

SNICKERDOODLE BROWNIES: Stir in 1 teaspoon ground cinnamon with flour. Omit nuts. After spreading batter in dish, sprinkle with mixture of 1 tablespoon sugar, heaping, and 1/2 teaspoon ground cinnamon.

CHOCOLATE CHEESECAKE BROWNIES

3 dozen brownies

Brownies:
2 cups sugar
1 cup margarine, melted
2/3 cup unsweetened cocoa powder
4 eggs
1 teaspoon vanilla extract
1 cup flour
1/2 teaspoon salt
Cheesecake Topping:
1 package (8 ounces) cream cheese, softened
2 tablespoons butter, softened
1 can (14 ounces) sweetened condensed milk
2 tablespoons sugar
1 egg
1 cup semisweet chocolate chips, melted
1 teaspoon vanilla extract

1. Heat oven to 350°. Line a 13x9x2-inch baking pan with aluminum foil. Spray with nonstick cooking spray; lightly flour.
2. Prepare brownies. Mix sugar, margarine, and cocoa in large bowl. Beat in eggs and vanilla. Stir in flour and salt. Spread in pan.
3. Prepare Cheesecake Topping. Beat cream cheese and butter with electric mixer on medium speed until light and fluffy. Beat in sweetened condensed milk and sugar, beating until smooth. Beat in egg, melted chocolate chips, and vanilla on low speed until combined. Carefully spoon cheesecake batter over brownie batter.
4. Bake 40 to 45 minutes or until cheesecake filling is firm.
5. Cool in pan on wire rack 45 minutes. Cover and refrigerate 8 hours or until well chilled. Cut into bars. Refrigerate any remaining brownies.

BUTTERSCOTCH CHEESECAKE BROWNIES: For Cheesecake Topping, omit sugar and substitute 1 cup butterscotch chips, melted, for semisweet chocolate chips.

PEANUT BUTTER CHEESECAKE BROWNIES: For Cheesecake Topping, omit sugar and substitute 1 cup peanut butter chips, melted, for semisweet chocolate chips.

TOFFEE CHEESECAKE BROWNIES: For Cheesecake Topping, omit sugar and decrease semisweet chocolate chips to 1/2 cup, melted. Stir in 1/2 cup butterscotch chips, melted, with the melted semisweet chocolate chips.

TOFFEE BROWNIES   16 brownies

1/2 cup butterscotch chips
1/2 cup semisweet chocolate chips
1/4 cup margarine, cut into pieces
1 cup packed light brown sugar
2 eggs
1 teaspoon vanilla extract
1 cup flour
1/2 teaspoon salt

1. Heat oven to 350°. Line a 9-inch square baking pan with aluminum foil. Spray with nonstick cooking spray; lightly flour.
2. Place butterscotch chips, chocolate chips, and margarine in microwavable bowl. Heat in microwave on High (100%), stopping and stirring, until mostly melted and smooth. Stir in brown sugar. Beat in eggs and vanilla. Stir in flour and salt. Spread in pan.
3. Bake 25 to 30 minutes or until toothpick inserted in center comes out clean. Cool in pan on wire rack. Cut into squares.

CANDIED FRUIT BARS   16 bars

Crust:
1 1/4 cups flour
1/4 cup sugar
1/8 teaspoon salt
1/2 cup cold margarine, cut into pieces
Filling:
3/4 cup mixed candied fruit, chopped
1/2 cup semisweet chocolate chips
2/3 cup sweetened condensed milk
1 teaspoon almond extract
1/4 cup chopped pecans

1. Heat oven to 350°. Spray a 9-inch square baking pan with nonstick cooking spray.
2. Mix flour, sugar, and salt in large bowl. Cut in margarine with fork until crumbly. Press firmly in bottom of pan. Bake 15 minutes.
3. Sprinkle with candied fruit and chocolate chips. Mix sweetened condensed milk and almond extract. Drizzle evenly over candied fruit and chocolate chips. Sprinkle with chopped pecans.
4. Bake 15 minutes or until light brown and bubbly. Cool in pan on wire rack. Cut into bars.

BANANA BROWNIES   16 brownies

1 cup sugar
1/2 cup margarine, melted
4 tablespoons unsweetened cocoa powder
2 eggs
1 teaspoon vanilla extract
3/4 cup flour
1/4 teaspoon baking powder
1/4 teaspoon salt
1/2 cup mashed banana
1/2 cup chopped banana
1/2 cup chopped pecans

1. Heat oven to 350°. Line an 8-inch square baking dish with aluminum foil. Spray with nonstick cooking spray; lightly flour.
2. Mix sugar, margarine, and cocoa in large bowl. Beat in eggs and vanilla. Stir in flour, baking powder, salt, and mashed banana. Stir in chopped banana and pecans. Spread in dish.
3. Bake 30 to 35 minutes or until toothpick inserted in center comes out clean. Cool in dish on wire rack. Cut into squares.

WHITE CHOCOLATE-ALMOND BLONDIES

25 bars

6 ounces white chocolate baking bar or squares, coarsely chopped
5 tablespoons margarine, cut into pieces
1 cup sugar
1 teaspoon vanilla extract
1/2 teaspoon almond extract
2 eggs
1 cup plus 2 tablespoons flour
1/2 teaspoon baking powder
1/4 teaspoon salt
3/4 cup white baking chips
1/4 cup sliced almonds
1 teaspoon flour
Garnish: 2 to 3 tablespoons sliced almonds

1. Heat oven to 350°. Line a 9-inch square baking pan with aluminum foil. Spray with nonstick cooking spray; lightly flour.
2. Place white chocolate and margarine in large microwavable bowl. Heat in microwave on Low (10%), stopping and stirring, until melted and smooth.
3. Stir in sugar, vanilla, and almond extract. Beat in eggs. Stir in flour, baking powder, and salt. Toss white baking chips, 1/4 cup sliced almonds, and 1 teaspoon flour in small bowl. Stir in chip mixture. Spread in pan. Sprinkle with 2 to 3 tablespoons sliced almonds.
4. Bake 30 to 40 minutes or until toothpick inserted in center comes out clean and Blondies are golden brown. Cool in pan on wire rack. Cut into bars.

PEANUT BUTTER BROWNIES 16 brownies

1/2 cup creamy peanut butter
1/4 cup margarine, softened
1 cup packed light brown sugar
2 eggs
1 teaspoon vanilla extract
1/2 cup flour
1/4 teaspoon salt
Frosting:
1/3 cup creamy peanut butter
3/4 cup powdered sugar
1 to 3 tablespoons milk

1. Heat oven to 350°. Line an 8-inch square baking dish with aluminum foil. Spray with nonstick cooking spray; lightly flour.
2. Mix peanut butter, margarine, and brown sugar in large bowl. Beat in eggs and vanilla. Stir in flour and salt. Spread in dish.
3. Bake 25 to 30 minutes or until toothpick inserted in center comes out clean. Cool in dish on wire rack.
4. Beat peanut butter and powdered sugar with electric mixer on low speed. Beat in 1 tablespoon milk on high speed. Gradually beat in additional milk until smooth and spreadable. Spread over brownies. Let stand until set. Lift brownies out of dish using aluminum foil. Cut into squares with hot knife.

PEANUT BUTTER-CHOCOLATE CHIP BROWNIES: Stir in 1 cup semisweet chocolate chips after stirring in flour and salt. Omit frosting, if desired.
PEANUT BUTTER AND JELLY BROWNIES: Omit frosting. After cooled, spread brownies with 1/3 to 1/2 cup warmed strawberry or raspberry preserves.

BROWNIE LIQUEUR PIE   6 servings

1 package (17.6 ounces) brownie mix or America's Best
  Brownies (page 162)
6 tablespoons chocolate-flavored syrup, room temperature
6 tablespoons liqueur (coffee-flavored, orange-flavored, amaretto,
  raspberry schnapps, or hazelnut)
Garnish: Whipped cream and shaved chocolate

1. Heat oven to 350°. Grease a 9-inch pie plate with shortening.
2. Mix brownie batter as directed; pour into pie plate. Bake 20
to 25 minutes. Cool 10 minutes in pie plate on wire rack. Cut warm pie
into 6 pieces.
3. Spoon 1 tablespoon chocolate-flavored syrup onto each of 6 small plates.
Place a pie piece on each plate. Drizzle 1 tablespoon liqueur over each pie
piece. Garnish with dollop of whipped cream and shaved chocolate.

LIME CREAM PIE   8 servings

Graham Cracker Crust for 9-inch pie (page 175 or purchased graham
  cracker crust)
1 package (8 ounces) cream cheese, softened
1 can (14 ounces) sweetened condensed milk
1/2 cup lime juice
2 teaspoons grated lime peel
3 drops green food color, if desired

1. Bake Graham Cracker Crust. Cool.
2. Beat cream cheese and sweetened condensed milk with electric mixer on
medium speed until smooth. Stir in lime juice, lime peel, and food color.
Turn filling into prepared pie crust.
3. Cover and refrigerate 2 to 3 hours or until firm. Refrigerate any remaining
pie.

LEMON CREAM PIE: Substitute lemon juice and lemon peel for lime
juice and lime peel. Substitute 6 drops yellow food color for green food
color.

ALOHA PIE   8 servings

1 package (15 ounces) refrigerated pie crusts or Two-Crust Pie
  (page 174)
Filling:
1/4 cup sugar
2 tablespoons flour
1 can (20 ounces) crushed pineapple in syrup
1 can (3 1/2 ounces) flaked coconut
1 cup white baking chips
1/2 cup chopped macadamia nuts or chopped almonds
2 tablespoons butter, melted
1 teaspoon imitation coconut extract
1/2 teaspoon almond extract
Garnish:
2 ounces white chocolate baking bar or squares, chopped
1 teaspoon shortening

1. Heat oven to 400°. Place 1 pastry in 9-inch pie plate; press firmly against
bottom and side. Cut remaining pastry into 1/2-inch strips.
2. Mix sugar and flour in large bowl. Stir in pineapple, coconut, white
baking chips, nuts, butter, coconut extract, and almond extract. Turn filling
into pastry-lined pie plate. Cover with lattice top. Press firmly around top
edge with tines of a fork. Cover top edge with strips of aluminum foil to
prevent excessive browning.
3. Bake 20 minutes. Remove aluminum foil strips and bake 30 to 40 minutes
longer or until light brown. Cool in pie plate on wire rack.
4. Place white chocolate baking bar and shortening in small microwavable
bowl. Heat in microwave on Low (10%), stopping and stirring, until smooth.
Pour mixture into a reclosable plastic bag. Snip a bottom corner of bag; pipe
mixture over pie.

WALNUT-PECAN PIE   8 servings

1 (9-inch) unbaked pie shell (page 174) or purchased pie shell
Filling:
1 cup light corn syrup
3/4 cup plus 2 tablespoons packed light brown sugar
1/3 cup margarine
3 eggs
1 tablespoon flour
1 teaspoon vanilla extract
Pinch of salt
1/2 cup chopped walnuts
1/2 cup chopped pecans

1. Heat corn syrup, brown sugar, and margarine to boiling in medium saucepan, stirring frequently. Remove from heat. Cool 30 minutes, stirring occasionally, to prevent a skin from developing on mixture.
2. Heat oven to 350°.
3. Place eggs, flour, vanilla, and salt in large bowl. Beat with electric mixer on low speed 1 minute. Pour warm syrup mixture into egg mixture, beating constantly on low speed until well combined. Stir in walnuts and pecans. Turn filling into pastry-lined 9-inch pie plate. Cover top edge with strips of aluminum foil to prevent excessive browning.
4. Bake 35 minutes. Remove aluminum foil strips and bake 5 to 10 minutes longer or until pie is uniformly set. Cool in pie plate on wire rack.

TEXAS PECAN PIE: Omit walnuts. Increase pecans to 1 cup. Stir in 1/2 cup semisweet chocolate chips with pecans. Turn filling into pastry-lined pie plate. Sprinkle with 1/2 cup semisweet chocolate chips.

KENTUCKY PECAN PIE: Prepare Texas Pecan Pie, adding 3 tablespoons bourbon to egg mixture.

BUTTERSCOTCH-PECAN APPLE PIE

8 servings

1 package (15 ounces) refrigerated pie crusts or Two-Crust
  Pie (page 174)
Filling:
1 can (20 ounces) sliced apples
2/3 cup packed light brown sugar
1 teaspoon imitation maple extract
3/4 teaspoon ground cinnamon
1/4 teaspoon salt
1/2 cup chopped pecans
1/2 cup butterscotch chips
2 tablespoons flour
2 tablespoons cold butter, cut into small pieces
Serve with: Vanilla ice cream

1. Heat oven to 425°. Place 1 pastry in 9-inch pie plate; press firmly against bottom and side. Cut remaining pastry into 1/2-inch strips.
2. Mix apples, brown sugar, maple extract, cinnamon, and salt in large bowl. Toss pecans, butterscotch chips, and flour in small bowl. Stir in pecan mixture. Turn filling into pastry-lined pie plate. Dot with butter pieces. Cover with lattice top. Press firmly around top edge with tines of a fork. Cover top edge with strips of aluminum foil to prevent excessive browning.
3. Bake 25 minutes. Remove aluminum foil strips and bake 5 to 10 minutes longer or until light brown. Serve warm with ice cream.

AFTER-DINNER MINT TART   8 servings

Crust:
1 1/2 cups chocolate cookie crumbs
5 tablespoons margarine, melted
Filling:
1 package (8 ounces) cream cheese, softened
1/3 cup plus 2 tablespoons sugar
1 egg
1/3 cup plus 1 tablespoon sour cream
1/4 teaspoon mint extract
Topping:
8 ounces semisweet chocolate, melted
3/4 cup sour cream
1/4 teaspoon mint extract

1. Heat oven to 300°. Mix crust ingredients. Press firmly on bottom of
a 9-inch springform pan.
2. Beat cream cheese until light and fluffy with electric mixer on medium
speed. Beat in sugar. Beat in egg, sour cream, and mint extract on low speed
until well combined. Pour over crust.
3. Bake 20 to 25 minutes or until filling is set, but not firm. Cool in pan on
wire rack 30 minutes. Cover and refrigerate 4 hours or until chilled.
4. Beat melted chocolate, sour cream, and mint extract until smooth and
spreadable. Remove side of springform pan. Spread topping over top and
side of tart, smoothing with knife. Chill 30 minutes or until set. Cut with hot
knife. Refrigerate any remaining tart.

ONE-CRUST PIE   1 (9-inch) pie crust

1 1/2 cups flour
1/4 teaspoon salt
1/2 cup shortening
1/4 cup cold water

1. Mix flour and salt. Cut in shortening with fork until crumbly. Sprinkle with cold water; toss with fork until all flour is moistened. Gather pastry into a ball.
2. Roll pastry into an 11- to 12-inch circle on lightly floured surface. Fold pastry in fourths; place in 9-inch pie plate. Unfold; press pastry firmly against bottom and side of plate. Trim overhanging edge of pastry even with top of plate. Press firmly around top edge with tines of fork.
3. Fill and bake as directed in pie recipe. For baked crust (unfilled), heat oven to 450°. Prick bottom and side of pastry with fork. Bake 8 to 12 minutes or until light brown; cool on wire rack.

TWO-CRUST PIE   2 (9-inch) pie crusts

2 1/4 cups flour
1/2 teaspoon salt, scant
3/4 cup shortening
6 to 7 tablespoons cold water

1. Mix as directed for One-Crust Pie. Divide pastry in half and shape into 2 balls.
2. Roll both pastry balls as directed in One-Crust Pie. Use one pastry to line a 9-inch pie plate. Use remaining pastry to cover filling. Press firmly around top edge with tines of a fork; cut slits so steam can escape. Or, create a lattice top. Cut pastry into 1/2-inch strips and place over filling. Press firmly around top edge with tines of fork.

GRAHAM CRACKER CRUST 1 (9-inch) pie crust

1 1/2 cups graham cracker crumbs
5 tablespoons margarine, melted

1. Heat oven to 350°.
2. Mix graham cracker crumbs and margarine with fork. Press against bottom and side of 9-inch pie plate. Do not place crumbs on rim.
3. Bake 5 minutes or until light brown; cool.

CHOCOLATE CRUMB CRUST: Substitute 1 1/2 cups chocolate cookie crumbs for graham cracker crumbs.

WHITE CHOCOLATE SHORTCAKE 4 servings

1 1/4 cups baking mix
3 tablespoons sugar
1 1/2 tablespoons margarine, melted
1/4 cup milk
1/2 teaspoon almond extract
3 ounces white chocolate baking bar or squares, coarsely chopped
Fresh strawberries, chopped
Sugar
Garnish: Shaved white chocolate

1. Heat oven to 425°. Line an 8-inch round cake pan with aluminum foil. Spray with nonstick cooking spray; lightly flour.
2. Mix baking mix, sugar, margarine, milk, and almond extract in medium bowl. Stir in white chocolate. Divide dough into 4 pieces and drop onto a lightly floured surface. With floured hands, shape each piece into a ball. Place in pan.
3. Bake 10 to 15 minutes or until light brown. Cool in pan on wire rack; remove with spatula to individual serving plates.
4. Mash chopped strawberries and sugar with fork. Spoon over shortcakes. Sprinkle shaved white chocolate over strawberries.

CANDY FRUITCAKE   1 loaf

4 cups graham cracker crumbs
1 cup raisins
1 cup chopped dates
1 cup mixed candied fruit, chopped
1 cup chopped pecans or walnuts
1 jar (7 1/2 ounces) marshmallow creme
1/2 cup milk

1. Line an 8 1/2-inch loaf dish with aluminum foil, letting aluminum foil extend about 5 inches above dish on 2 sides. Spray with nonstick cooking spray.
2. Mix graham cracker crumbs, raisins, dates, candied fruit, and nuts in large bowl.
3. Melt marshmallow creme and milk over low heat in a stockpot, stirring frequently, until smooth. Remove from heat; stir in graham cracker mixture. Mix thoroughly. Press firmly in dish. Cover and refrigerate 48 hours to blend flavors.
4. Lift fruitcake out of dish onto a cutting board and peel back the aluminum foil from the sides before cutting. Refrigerator any remaining fruitcake.

FLOURLESS CHOCOLATE CAKE   6 servings

4 ounces semisweet chocolate, cut into pieces
1/2 cup butter, cut into pieces
2/3 cup sugar
3 eggs
1/3 cup unsweetened cocoa powder
Garnish: Powdered sugar

1. Heat oven to 375°. Line the bottom of an 8-inch springform pan with aluminum foil.* Spray pan with nonstick cooking spray.
2. Place chocolate in microwavable bowl. Heat in microwave on High (100%) 30 seconds. Add butter; heat on High (100%), stopping and stirring, until chocolate and butter are melted and smooth. Stir in sugar. Beat in eggs. Sift cocoa over batter; stir vigorously until well combined. Pour into pan.

176

3. Bake 20 to 25 minutes or until top develops a thin crust. Cool 5 minutes in pan on wire rack. Remove side of pan; cool completely. The cake will fall while cooling. Sprinkle with powdered sugar.

*An 8-inch round cake pan can be substituted. Line pan with aluminum foil, letting aluminum foil extend above pan. Trim aluminum foil with scissors to extend height about 1 inch.

CRANBERRY UPSIDE-DOWN CAKE   9 servings

2 tablespoons butter, cut into pieces
1/3 cup packed light brown sugar
1 1/2 cups whole berry cranberry sauce, broken up
Cake:
1 1/2 cups baking mix
1/2 cup sugar
1 egg
1/2 cup milk
2 tablespoons shortening
1 teaspoon vanilla extract
1/2 teaspoon orange extract

1. Heat oven to 350°. Melt butter in a 9-inch cake pan. Sprinkle brown sugar over butter. Spoon cranberry sauce over brown sugar.
2. Beat all cake ingredients in medium bowl with electric mixer on medium speed until combined. Beat on medium speed 2 minutes. Spoon batter into pan over cranberry sauce.
3. Bake 35 to 40 minutes or until toothpick inserted in center comes out clean. Loosen side of cake from pan. Immediately invert pan onto a heat-proof plate; leave pan over cake 2 minutes while topping drains over cake. Remove pan. Serve warm or cool.

BLUEBERRY UPSIDE-DOWN CAKE
Substitute 1 1/2 cups blueberry pie filling for the cranberry sauce and 1/2 teaspoon almond extract for the orange extract.

CHERRY UPSIDE-DOWN CAKE
Prepare Blueberry Upside-Down Cake substituting cherry pie filling for the blueberry pie filling.

EGGNOG LOAF CAKE   1 loaf cake

1/2 cup margarine, melted
1 cup sugar
1 egg
2 tablespoons dark rum
1 1/2 teaspoons imitation rum extract
1 teaspoon vanilla extract
2 1/4 cups flour
1 tablespoon baking powder
1 teaspoon ground nutmeg
1/2 teaspoon salt
1 cup milk
Eggnog Glaze (below)

1. Heat oven to 350°. Spray an 8 1/2-inch loaf dish with nonstick cooking spray; lightly flour.
2. Beat margarine, sugar, egg, rum, rum extract, and vanilla in large bowl with electric mixer on low speed. Mix flour, baking powder, nutmeg, and salt in small bowl. Beat flour mixture and milk alternately into sugar mixture on low speed. Pour into dish.
3. Bake 50 to 60 minutes or until toothpick inserted in center comes out clean. Cool 10 minutes in dish on wire rack. Loosen side of loaf from dish; remove from dish and place top side up on wire rack. Cool completely.
4. Drizzle with Eggnog Glaze.

EGGNOG GLAZE

1 cup powdered sugar
3 to 4 teaspoons milk
1/2 teaspoon imitation rum extract

Mix all ingredients until smooth and thin enough to drizzle.

AUSTRIAN HAZELNUT TORTE   10 servings

1 package (18 ounces) refrigerated sugar cookie dough
Filling:
1 package (8 ounces) cream cheese, softened
1/3 cup packed light brown sugar
1 teaspoon imitation maple extract
1/2 teaspoon ground cinnamon
1 egg
1 cup chopped hazelnuts or pecans
Garnish: 2 to 3 tablespoons chopped hazelnuts or pecans

1. Line the bottom of a 9-inch springform pan with aluminum foil. Spray with nonstick cooking spray.
2. Divide sugar cookie dough in half. Cut one half into 1/4-inch slices. With floured hands, press dough slices on bottom and 1/2 inch up side of pan. Form remaining dough into a ball; flatten into a circle. Roll out dough between 2 sheets of waxed paper into a 10-inch circle. Place in freezer to firm.
3. Heat oven to 350°. Beat cream cheese until light and fluffy with electric mixer on medium speed. Beat in brown sugar, maple extract, and cinnamon. Beat in egg on low speed. Stir in hazelnuts. Pour into pan.
4. Remove dough from freezer. Peel off top wax paper; carefully invert into pan. Peel off remaining sheet of wax paper. Fit dough into pan, pressing gently with fingertips. Trim excess dough. Don't worry if dough cracks. Cracks disappear after baking. Sprinkle with chopped nuts, pressing to adhere.
5. Bake 30 to 35 minutes or until top is light brown. Cool in pan on wire rack. Cover and chill 8 hours to blend flavors.
6. Serve at room temperature. Remove side of pan and slice. Refrigerate any remaining cake.

CHOCOLATE-SPECKLED CAKE   10 servings

1/3 cup butter, softened
3/4 cup plus 2 tablespoons sugar
2 eggs, separated
1 teaspoon vanilla extract
1/4 teaspoon imitation coconut extract
1/4 teaspoon almond extract
1 1/2 cups flour
1 1/2 teaspoons baking powder
1/4 teaspoon salt
2/3 cup milk
2 ounces semisweet chocolate, grated
Chocolate Cream Cheese Frosting (below)

1. Heat oven to 350°. Line the bottom of a 9-inch springform pan with aluminum foil. Spray pan with nonstick cooking spray; lightly flour.
2. Beat butter and sugar in large bowl with electric mixer. Beat in egg yolks, vanilla, coconut extract, and almond extract. Mix flour, baking powder, and salt in small bowl. Beat flour mixture and milk alternately into sugar mixture on low speed. Stir in grated chocolate.
3. Beat egg whites with electric mixer on high speed until stiff; fold into batter. Spread in pan.
4. Bake 25 to 30 minutes or until toothpick inserted in center comes out with only a moist crumb. Cool in pan 10 minutes on wire rack. Remove side of pan; cool completely. Cover and store overnight to blend flavors.
5. Prepare frosting. Split cake in half, making two layers. Spread frosting on cut side of bottom layer. Place remaining half, cut side down, on frosting. Frost top and side of cake. Serve at room temperature. Refrigerate any remaining cake.

CHOCOLATE CREAM CHEESE FROSTING

1 package (8 ounces) cream cheese, softened
3 to 3 1/2 cups sifted powdered sugar
4 ounces semisweet chocolate, melted
1 teaspoon vanilla extract
1 to 2 teaspoons milk

Beat cream cheese, 3 cups powdered sugar, melted chocolate, vanilla, and 1 teaspoon milk in medium bowl with electric mixer until smooth. Gradually beat in additional sugar or milk until smooth and spreadable.

MINT CHOCOLATE FUDGE CHEESECAKE

12 to 18 servings

Crust:
1 1/2 cups chocolate cookie crumbs
3 tablespoons margarine, melted
Filling:
3 packages (8 ounces each) cream cheese, softened
2/3 cup sugar
4 eggs
1 can (14 ounces) sweetened condensed milk
2 cups semisweet chocolate chips, melted
1 teaspoon mint extract
Topping:
1 cup semisweet chocolate chips, melted
1/2 cup sour cream
1/4 teaspoon mint extract, scant

NOTE:
Cheesecakes are easy-to-prepare, but take more time than many other desserts. Your reward for the extra effort is a heavenly, scrumptious creation.

1. Heat oven to 300°. Mix crust ingredients. Press firmly on bottom of a 9-inch springform pan.
2. Beat cream cheese until light and fluffy in large bowl with electric mixer on medium speed. Gradually beat in sugar. Add eggs, one at a time, beating on low speed until blended. Beat in sweetened condensed milk, melted chocolate chips, and mint extract on low speed until well combined. Pour filling over crust.
3. Bake 50 to 60 minutes. Cheesecake is done when it springs back when lightly touched in the center (cheesecake will shake slightly when moved). Remove cake from oven and run a knife around the inside edge of the pan.
4. Cool in pan on wire rack 1 hour. Cover and refrigerate 8 hours or overnight.
5. Stir melted chocolate chips and sour cream in small bowl. Stir in mint extract. Remove side of pan. Spread evenly over top of cheesecake. Chill 20 to 30 minutes or until topping is set. Refrigerate any remaining cheesecake.

IRISH CREAM-CHOCOLATE CHEESECAKE

12 to 18 servings

Crust:
1 1/2 cups chocolate cookie crumbs
3 tablespoons margarine, melted
Irish Cream Filling:
3 packages (8 ounces each) cream cheese, softened
1 1/4 cups sugar
3 eggs
1/2 cup sour cream
3/4 cup Irish cream liqueur
Chocolate Filling:
2 1/3 cups Irish Cream Filling
3 tablespoons unsweetened cocoa powder
3 tablespoons sugar

1. Heat oven to 300°. Mix crust ingredients. Press firmly on bottom of a 9-inch springform pan.
2. Beat cream cheese until light and fluffy in large bowl with electric mixer on medium speed. Gradually beat in sugar. Add eggs, one at a time, beating on low speed until blended. Beat in sour cream and Irish cream liqueur on low speed until well combined.
3. For chocolate filling transfer 2 1/3 cups Irish cream filling to medium bowl. Beat in cocoa and sugar with electric mixer on low speed.
Remove 2/3 cup chocolate filling and reserve. This will be used to create the marble design on the top of the cheesecake.
4. Pour one-third Irish cream filling over crust. Drop large spoonfuls of the chocolate filling over the Irish cream filling. Gently spoon remaining Irish cream filling into pan. Drop spoonfuls of the reserved chocolate filling into pan. Cut through mixtures with knife for marble effect.
5. Bake 45 to 55 minutes. Cheesecake is done when it springs back when lightly touched in the center (cheesecake will shake slightly when moved). Remove cake from oven and run a knife around inside edge of pan.
6. Cool in pan on wire rack 1 hour. Cover and refrigerate 8 hours or until chilled. Refrigerate any remaining cheesecake.

NUTELLA CHEESECAKE   10 to 16 servings

Crust:
1 1/4 cups graham cracker crumbs
2 tablespoons sugar
1/4 cup margarine, softened
Filling:
2 packages (8 ounces each) cream cheese, softened
3/4 cup sugar, scant
2 eggs
1/2 cup sour cream
1/3 cup Nutella®
1 teaspoon vanilla extract
Topping:
4 tablespoons Nutella®
3 tablespoons sugar
1 1/4 cups sour cream
1 teaspoon vanilla extract
Garnish: Nutella® and 1/2 cup finely chopped hazelnuts or pecans

NOTE:
Nutella® is a chocolate-hazelnut spread available in large supermarkets (usually located near the peanut butter).

1. Heat oven to 300°. Mix all crust ingredients. Press firmly on bottom of a 9-inch springform pan.
2. Beat cream cheese until light and fluffy in large bowl with electric mixer on medium speed. Gradually beat in sugar. Add eggs, one at a time, beating on low speed until blended. Beat in sour cream, Nutella, and vanilla on low speed until well combined. Pour filling over crust.
3. Bake 45 to 55 minutes. Cheesecake is done when it springs back when lightly touched in the center (cheesecake will shake slightly when moved).
4. Remove cake from the oven. Beat Nutella and sugar in small bowl with electric mixer. Beat in sour cream and vanilla. Spread evenly over top of cheesecake. Bake 3 to 5 minutes longer or until topping is set. Remove cake from the oven and run a knife around the inside edge of the pan.
5. Cool in pan on wire rack 1 hour. Refrigerate uncovered 8 hours or overnight.
6. Remove side of pan. Spread a thin layer of Nutella on side of cheesecake; press chopped nuts into Nutella. Refrigerate any remaining cheesecake.

BUTTERED PECAN CHEESECAKE

12 to 18 servings

Crust:
1 1/2 cups graham cracker crumbs
1/2 cup chopped buttered pecans (page 185)
1/4 cup packed light brown sugar
3 tablespoons butter, melted
Filling:
3 packages (8 ounces each) cream cheese, softened
1 1/4 cups packed light brown sugar
3 eggs
1 cup sour cream
2 teaspoons imitation maple extract
1 cup chopped buttered pecans
Garnish: Whipped cream and chopped buttered pecans

1. Heat oven to 300°. Mix all crust ingredients. Press firmly on bottom and halfway up side of a 9-inch springform pan.
2. Beat cream cheese until light and fluffy in large bowl with electric mixer on medium speed. Gradually beat in brown sugar. Add eggs, one at a time, beating on low speed until blended. Beat in sour cream and maple extract on low speed until well combined.
3. Pour one-third filling over crust. Sprinkle evenly with 1/3 cup pecans. Gently spoon one-third filling over pecans. Sprinkle again with 1/3 cup pecans. Gently spoon remaining filling over pecans. Sprinkle with 1/3 cup pecans.
4. Bake 50 to 60 minutes. Cheesecake is done when it springs back when lightly touched in center (cheesecake will shake slightly when moved). Remove cake from oven and run a knife around the inside edge of the pan.
5. Cool in pan on wire rack 1 hour; cover and refrigerate 8 hours or until chilled.
6. Remove side of pan. Garnish rim of cheesecake with dollops of whipped cream. Sprinkle whipped cream with chopped buttered pecans. Refrigerate any remaining cheesecake.

BUTTERED PECANS   2 cups

2 tablespoons plus 2 teaspoons butter
2 cups chopped pecans
Salt

1. Melt butter in large skillet over medium heat, heating until foam subsides. Cook pecans in butter 5 minutes, stirring occasionally, until pecans are golden brown.
2. Drain on paper towel. Sprinkle lightly with salt. Cool to room temperature. Refrigerate unused nuts.

7
SUBSTITUTIONS
AND EQUIVALENTS

Are you missing an important ingredient for a recipe? Eliminate frustration and time consuming shopping by using a substitution or equivalent ingredient.

Although in most cases I prefer to use the original ingredient, the following list has proven invaluable to me on many occasions.

BAKING

1 cup cake flour	1 cup minus 2 tablespoons all-purpose flour
1 cup self-rising flour	1 cup all-purpose flour, 1 1/2 teaspoons baking powder, and 1/2 teaspoon salt
1 cup bread flour	1 cup all-purpose flour and 1 teaspoon wheat gluten
Baking mix	5 cups all-purpose flour, 1/4 cup sugar, 2 tablespoons plus 2 teaspoons baking powder, 1 1/2 teaspoons salt, and 1 cup shortening. Combine dry ingredients; cut in shortening with fork until crumbly (6 cups). Store in refrigerator in airtight container; use within 3 months.
1 teaspoon baking powder	1/4 teaspoon baking soda and 1/2 teaspoon cream of tartar
1 cup self-rising cornmeal	1 cup yellow or white cornmeal, 1 1/2 teaspoons baking powder, and 1/2 teaspoon salt
1 cup powdered sugar	1 cup sugar and 1 tablespoon cornstarch. Process in food processor until very fine.
1 cup sugar	2 cups powdered sugar, sifted
1 cup packed light brown sugar	1/2 cup sugar and 1/2 cup packed dark brown sugar
1 cup packed light brown sugar	1 cup sugar and 1 to 2 tablespoons molasses or dark corn syrup

1 cup light corn syrup	1 cup sugar and 1/4 cup water or liquid used in recipe (except for making candy)
1 cup honey	1 1/4 cups sugar and 1/4 cup water or liquid used in recipe
13 to 15 squares graham crackers (1 cup crumbs)	24 to 26 vanilla wafers (1 cup crumbs)
1 egg	1/4 cup liquid egg substitute. Or, 1/4 cup silk tofu, pureed. Or, 3 tablespoons mayonnaise.

DAIRY

1 cup buttermilk	1 cup milk and 1 tablespoon white vinegar or lemon juice. Mix; let stand at room temperature 5 minutes.
2 cups whipped cream (1 cup heavy cream, unwhipped)	2 cups non-dairy whipped topping, thawed
1 cup heavy cream, unwhipped	3/4 cup whole milk and 1/3 cup butter, melted
1 cup light cream (half-and-half)	7/8 cup whole milk and 3 tablespoons butter, melted
1 cup whole milk	1/2 cup water and 1/2 cup evaporated milk
1 cup whole milk	1 cup skim milk and 2 teaspoons butter
1 cup skim milk	1/3 cup nonfat dry milk and 1 cup water
1 cup eggnog	1 cup half-and-half, 1/4 teaspoon ground nutmeg, and 1/2 teaspoon imitation rum extract
1 cup coconut milk	1 cup heavy cream, 1/2 teaspoon sugar, and 1/2 teaspoon imitation coconut extract
1 cup sour cream	1 cup heavy cream and 1 tablespoon lemon juice or white vinegar. Mix; let stand at room temperature 30 to 60 minutes to thicken.
1 cup sour cream	1 cup yogurt (Add 1 tablespoon cornstarch when using yogurt to prepare a cooked sauce.)
14-ounce can sweetened condensed milk	1 cup nonfat dry milk, 3/4 cup sugar, 1/3 cup boiling water, and 1 tablespoon butter, melted. Place ingredients in blender. Blend 3 to 5 minutes or until thick and smooth. Cover and refrigerate until mixture is thickened. Store in refrigerator.

| 8 ounces cream cheese | 1 cup low-fat cottage cheese, drained, and 4 tablespoons margarine. Process in food processor until smooth. Cover and refrigerate until mixture is thickened. |

CHOCOLATE

1-ounce square unsweetened chocolate, melted	3 tablespoons unsweetened cocoa powder and 1 tablespoon shortening or margarine, melted
1-ounce square semisweet chocolate, melted	1 ounce unsweetened chocolate, melted, and 4 teaspoons sugar
6-ounce package semisweet chocolate chips, melted	2 ounces unsweetened chocolate, melted, 7 tablespoons sugar, and 2 tablespoons shortening, melted
6 ounces semisweet chocolate, melted	6-ounce package semisweet chocolate chips (1 cup), melted
3 ounces bittersweet chocolate, melted	2 ounces semisweet chocolate, melted, and 1 ounce unsweetened chocolate, melted
4 ounces sweet baking chocolate	3 tablespoons unsweetened cocoa, 4 1/2 tablespoons sugar, and 2 2/3 tablespoons shortening

SPICES/HERBS

1 tablespoon chopped fresh herb	1 teaspoon dried leaf herb
1 tablespoon prepared mustard	1 teaspoon dry mustard
1 teaspoon Italian seasoning	1/4 teaspoon dried thyme leaves, 1/4 teaspoon dried oregano leaves, 1/4 teaspoon dried basil leaves, and 1/4 teaspoon dried marjoram leaves
1/8 teaspoon ground red pepper (cayenne)	4 drops Tabasco
1 teaspoon hot pepper sauce	3/4 teaspoon red pepper (cayenne) and 1 teaspoon white vinegar
1 garlic clove	1/8 teaspoon garlic powder
1 teaspoon garlic salt	1/8 teaspoon garlic powder and 7/8 teaspoon salt

188

1/2 teaspoon grated fresh ginger	1/4 teaspoon ground ginger
1 teaspoon apple pie spice	1/2 teaspoon ground cinnamon, 1/4 teaspoon ground nutmeg, 1/8 teaspoon ground allspice, and dash ground cloves or ground ginger
1 teaspoon pumpkin pie spice	1/2 teaspoon ground cinnamon, 1/4 teaspoon ground ginger, 1/8 teaspoon nutmeg, and 1/8 teaspoon ground cloves
1 teaspoon allspice	1/2 teaspoon ground cinnamon, 1/4 teaspoon ground cloves, and 1/4 teaspoon ground ginger
Blackened seasoning	1 1/2 tablespoons dried oregano leaves, 1 tablespoon dried thyme leaves, 1 tablespoon paprika, 1 tablespoon garlic powder, 1 tablespoon onion powder, 1 tablespoon salt, 1 tablespoon coarse black pepper, 1/4 teaspoon ground red pepper (cayenne), or to taste
Jerk seasoning	1/2 teaspoon garlic powder, 1/2 teaspoon allspice, 1/2 teaspoon dried thyme leaves, 1/8 teaspoon ground red pepper (cayenne) or black pepper, 1/8 teaspoon salt, and 1/8 teaspoon sugar
Cajun seasoning	3 tablespoons paprika, 2 tablespoons garlic powder, 1 tablespoon salt, 1 tablespoon onion powder, 1 tablespoon dried thyme leaves, 1 tablespoon coarse black pepper, and 1/4 teaspoon red pepper (cayenne), or to taste

MISCELLANEOUS

1 anchovy fillet	1/2 teaspoon anchovy paste
1 tablespoon nuoc nam (Asian fish sauce)	2 teaspoons soy sauce and 1 teaspoon anchovy paste
1/2 pound fresh mushrooms	6 ounces canned mushrooms, drained
1 pound fresh mushrooms, sliced	3 ounces dried mushrooms
1/4 cup chopped onion	1 tablespoon dried minced onion
2 cups tomato sauce	6-ounce can tomato paste and 1 1/2 cups water
1 cup tomato juice	1/2 cup tomato sauce and 1/2 cup water
Ketchup	8-ounce can tomato sauce, 1/4 cup sugar, and 3 tablespoons white vinegar. Combine all ingredients; heat until sugar is dissolved and mixture is thickened.

1 tablespoon cornstarch (used as thickening agent in cooked sauces)	2 tablespoons flour
1/2 cup honey mustard	1/4 cup honey and 1/4 cup Dijon mustard
20-ounce can crushed pineapple in heavy syrup	20-ounce can crushed pineapple in juice, drained (press out as much juice as possible), with juice reserved. Heat juice and 1/2 cup sugar until sugar is dissolved. Remove from heat. Add crushed pineapple. Let stand 10 minutes.

FISH SUBSTITUTION TABLE

One type of fish can be substituted for another when preparing recipes. Refer to the following table for suitable choices.

Species	Substitute
Catfish	Amberjack, Orange Roughy, Tilapia, Rockfish
Cod	Haddock, Lingcod, Pollock
Flounder	Ocean Perch, Pompano, Sole, Whiting
Halibut	Black Sea Bass, Mahi-mahi (Dolphin Fish, Dorado), Striped Sea Bass, Turbot
Orange Roughy	Catfish, Cod, Haddock, Pollock, Tilapia
Red Snapper	Black Sea Bass, Grouper, Mahi-mahi, Monkfish, Pacific Rockfish, Porgy
Salmon	Artic Char (Trout), Lake Trout, Rainbow Trout, Steelhead Trout, Whitefish
Tuna	Blue Marlin, Ono (Wahoo), Shark, Swordfish

BAKING PAN SUBSTITUTIONS

Refer to the following table when you don't have the pan that a recipe recommends. Altering the pan size or shape will change the baking time, so watch your oven carefully while you are baking.

Recommended Baking Pan	Substitution
8-inch round cake pan	9-inch pie plate
9-inch round cake pan	10-inch pie plate or 8-inch square pan
2 9-inch round cake pans	2 medium muffin pans (2 1/2 x 1 1/4-inches per muffin)--i.e., yields 24 cupcakes
13x9x2-inch pan	Two 9-inch round cake pans or two 8-inch square pans
11x7-inch pan	9-inch square pan
9-inch square pan	15x10x1-inch jelly roll pan
10x4-inch tube pan	Two 8-inch square pans or two 9x5x3-inch loaf pans
9x5x3-inch loaf pan	Two 7 1/2 x 3 3/4 x 2 1/4-inch loaf pans or three 5 1/2 x 3 1/4 x 2 1/4-inch loaf pans
8 1/2 x 4 1/2 x 2 1/2-inch loaf pan	Two 5 1/2 x 3 1/4 x 2 1/4-inch loaf pans or one 1-pound coffee can

METRIC EQUIVALENTS

Grocery shopping in Canada and Mexico is confusing unless you are familiar with metric equivalents. If you buy a cookbook while traveling, converting metric recipes can also be difficult. The following lists will assist in your shopping and cooking.

LIQUID AND SPOON MEASUREMENTS

1/4 teaspoon = 1 ml
1/2 teaspoon = 2 ml
3/4 teaspoon = 4 ml
1 teaspoon = 5 ml
1 tablespoon (1/2 ounce) = 15 ml
2 tablespoons (1 ounce) = 30 ml
1/4 cup (2 ounces) = 60 ml
1/3 cup (3 1/3 ounces) = 75 ml
1/2 cup (4 ounces) = 125 ml
3/4 cup (6 ounces) = 175 ml
1 cup (8 ounces) = 250 ml
2 cups (1 pint) = 500 ml
3 cups = 750 ml
1 quart (4 cups) = 950 ml
1 gallon = 3.8 liters

DRY WEIGHT

1/2 ounce (1 tablespoon) = 15 g
1 ounce (2 tablespoons) = 30 g
4 ounces (1/4 pound) = 120 g
8 ounces (1/2 pound) = 225 g
12 ounces (3/4 pound) = 360 g
16 ounces (1 pound) = 450 g
2 1/4 pounds = 1 kilogram
1 cup (4 ounces) flour = 150 g
1 cup (8 ounces) sugar = 225 g
1 cup (8 ounces/1/2 pound/
  2 sticks) butter = 225 g

OVEN TEMPERATURES

°F	°C	Gas	°F	°C	Gas
250	130	1/2	400	200	6
275	140	1	425	220	7
300	150	2	450	230	8
325	160	3	475	240	9
350	180	4	500	260	--
375	190	5	Broil		Grill

STANDARD MEASUREMENTS

1 tablespoon = 3 teaspoons
2 tablespoons = 1 ounce
1/4 cup = 4 tablespoons
1/3 cup = 5 1/3 tablespoons
1/2 cup = 8 tablespoons
1 cup = 16 tablespoons/
   8 fluid ounces

1/2 pint = 1 cup/
   8 fluid ounces
1 pint = 2 cups
1 pound = 16 ounces
1 quart = 2 pints
1 gallon = 4 quarts

BASIC RECIPES

Remote areas might not stock all of your favorite products. The following recipes prove useful when you are in an area that does not have an essential ingredient.

Preparing basic foods from scratch requires time and energy. However, if you enjoy cooking, you will enjoy the following recipes. Freshly made, quality products are your reward.

BREADS/GRAINS

Pizza Crust, page 42
Polenta, page 142
Tortillas, page 39

SAUCES

Alfredo Sauce, page 117
Cocktail Sauce, page 81
Enchilada Sauce, page 118
Pesto, page 141
Picante Sauce, page 90
Tartar Sauce, page 84
Salsa, page 16
Spaghetti Sauce, page 118
White Sauce, page 117

PIES

Chocolate Crumb
   Crust, page 175
Graham Cracker
   Crust, page 175
Pie Crust, page 174

TIMESAVERS

Save time and energy at mealtime by letting someone else do the work for you. Keep prepared ingredients on hand for quick-and-easy preparation. These shortcut products can provide variety without sacrificing flavor. Look over the following list and choose your favorites. Convenience foods make helpful additions to your basic pantry list.

BREADS
Bread and muffin mixes
Corn bread mix
Frozen bread dough and rolls
Prepared pizza crust
Refrigerated pastry dough

DESSERTS
Angel food cake
Brownie and cookie mixes
Cake mix
Chocolate cookie crumb pie crust
Frozen pies, cobblers, and cakes
Fruit pie filling
Graham cracker crumbs
Graham cracker crumb pie crust
Store-bought cookies
Pound cake
Prepared pie shells
Pudding and pie filling mix
Ready-made bakery desserts
Refrigerated cookie dough

MAIN DISHES
Canned chicken
Frozen hamburger patties
Frozen meatballs
Packaged casserole mixes
Pre-cooked shrimp

SAUCES
Alfredo sauce
Barbecue sauce
Bottled marinades
Canned cream soups
Canned gravies
Cocktail sauce
Dry sauce mixes
Pesto
Picante sauce
Pizza sauce
Ready-made pasta sauces
Tartar sauce
Teriyaki sauce
Salsa
Seasoned canned tomatoes
Stir-fry sauce
Sweet-and-sour sauce

SEASONINGS
Barbecue seasoning
Blackened seasoning
Bottled garlic
Cajun seasoning
Dry onion soup mix
Dry salad dressing mix
Fajita seasoning
Jerk seasoning
Italian seasoning
Taco seasoning mix
Grilled meat seasonings

SIDE DISHES
Deli salads
Fresh pasta
Frozen mixed vegetables
Frozen vegetables with sauce
Instant couscous, polenta,
   potatoes, and rice
Packaged coleslaw mixtures
Packaged salad mixtures
Canned/jarred salad mixtures
Pre-cut fruits and vegetables
Pre-shredded cheese

8
COMMON PROBLEMS

Dealing with the aridity of Arizona, the extreme humidity of Louisiana, and the high altitude of New Mexico can be challenging. This chapter alerts you to possible cooking problems that you might encounter due to extreme climates or high altitude. The following practical advice will enable you to successfully cope with these difficulties.

DRYNESS
Arid desert air can quickly dry out your ingredients and prepared foods. Prevent dryness by taking the following precautionary measures:

- Use an airtight container for all items stored at room temperature.
- Store loaf/sandwich bread in the refrigerator or a cooler.
- Place an apple slice or slice of bread in your brown sugar container. Seal tightly, then store in the refrigerator or a cooler.
- Double bag items that you package for the freezer.
- Place an apple slice or a folded damp paper towel in containers holding home baked goods (cakes, cookies, breads, etc.) that are stored at room temperature.
- Rice requires additional liquid when prepared in dry climates. Watch carefully to avoid evaporation.
- Oven casseroles and main dishes with sauces require additional liquid when baked uncovered in dry climates. Watch carefully to avoid evaporation.

HUMIDITY

A damp climate can be annoying as well as physically uncomfortable. The excessive moisture causes crackers to get soggy, bakery goods to mildew, and bugs to proliferate. The following tips will help minimize these problems:

- Place all foods stored at room temperature in airtight containers.
- Crisp soggy crackers by baking in 275° oven for 20 to 30 minutes.
- Store loaf/sandwich bread in the refrigerator or a cooler to prevent mildew.
- Prevent bug and worms from developing in flour, cereal, and rice by wrapping the package in plastic wrap and freezing for 24 hours. Thaw without opening.
- Avoid bugs by keeping food preparation area as clean and dry as possible.
- When making candy increase the cooking time to compensate for extra moisture.

HIGH ALTITUDE

When preparing foods at high altitude (altitudes greater than 3000 feet), adjustments must be made. Oven casseroles and roasted meats usually take longer to bake. Increase the oven temperature by 25° or increase the baking time, starting with 5 minutes. Foods that are boiled and foods containing leavening ingredients are the major concerns.

Boiling

At sea level, water boils at 212°. As altitude increases, the boiling temperature drops (about 1° for each 500-foot increase). In other words, a boiling liquid at 5000 feet is not as hot as a boiling liquid at 3000 feet. Because it is heat that cooks food, not "boiling," compensate for the lower temperature by increasing the cooking time. More liquid may be required since evaporation is increased.

For example, at 3000 feet I simmer stew for 2 1/2 hours, but at 5000 feet I increase the time to 3 hours. Experimentation will determine the correct cooking time and the amount of additional liquid needed.

Candy preparation is the exception. Because evaporation increases at high altitudes, the candy mixture will become concentrated and "sugary" if cooked longer. It will reach soft ball stage, hard ball stage, etc. faster than it will at normal altitude.

Ultimately, there is not an exact formula to follow. Experimentation yields the best results.

Leavening

Atmospheric pressure decreases as altitude increases. Essentially, this means that as air becomes thinner, foods containing leavening ingredients will rise faster and more easily.

Recipes containing yeast as a leavening agent do not require adjustment. However, they will take less time to rise than at normal altitude.

If baking powder or baking soda is used, adjustments are necessary. The table below provides helpful, general guidelines. When two amounts are listed, try the smaller amount first. If your recipe uses baking soda and baking powder, reduce both ingredients. In recipes that use baking soda, never reduce below one-half teaspoon for every cup of sour milk.

When baking cakes and non-yeast breads, increase the oven temperature 25°. The higher temperature stabilizes the batter and prevents falling.

ADJUSTMENT	3000 feet	5000 feet	7000 feet
Reduce baking powder/ baking soda. For each teaspoon, decrease:	1/8 tsp.	1/8 to 1/4 tsp.	1/4 tsp.
Reduce sugar. For each cup, decrease:	0 to 1 Tbs.	0 to 2 Tbs.	1 to 3 Tbs.
Increase liquid. For each cup, add:	1 to 2 Tbs.	2 to 4 Tbs.	3 to 4 Tbs.
Increase flour. For each cup, add:	0 to 1 Tbs.	1 to 2 Tbs.	2 to 3 Tbs.

(Table courtesy of Cooperative Extension Service of New Mexico State University)

RESOURCES

CAMPGROUND INFORMATION

COLEMAN NATIONAL FOREST CAMPGROUND AND
RECREATION DIRECTORY by Coleman Company and Our Forests,
Inc. The Globe Pequot Press, P.O. Box 480, Guilford, Connecticut
06437 1-888-249-7586 www.globe-pequot.com

THE COMPLETE GUIDE TO AMERICA'S NATIONAL PARKS, by
Pamela Wiesen, ed. Fodor's Travel Publications www.fodors.com

NATIONAL FOREST SERVICE, P.O. Box 96090, Washington, D.C.
20090 202-205-8333 www.fs.fed.us

NATIONAL GEOGRAPHIC GUIDE TO NATIONAL PARKS OF THE
UNITED STATES by the Book Division. National Geographic Society,
Washington, D.C. 1-800-437-5521 www.nationalgeographic.com

NATIONAL PARK SERVICE, 1849 C Street, NW, Washington, D.C.
20240 For campground reservations 1-800-365-2267 www.nps.gov

NATIONAL REFUGES, U.S. Fish & Wildlife Service, Public Affairs
Office, 1849 C Street, NW, Publication Dep. WEB, Room 130,
Washington, D.C. 20240 703-358-1711 www.refuges.fws.gov

TRAILER LIFE DIRECTORY: CAMPGROUNDS, RV PARKS AND
SERVICES by TL Enterprises. Trailer Life Campground/RV Parks and
Services Directory, P.O. Box 10236, Des Moines, Iowa 50382 1-800-
234-3450 www.tldirectory.com

WOODALL'S THE CAMPGROUND DIRECTORY by Woodall, ed.
Woodall Publications Corp., 2575 Vista Del Mar Drive, Ventura,
California 93001 1-800-323-9076 www.woodalls.com

RV COOKBOOKS

CAMPING CUISINE by Marie Royer. Mossy Creek Publishing,
   P.O. Box 50361, Eugene, Oregon 97405

COOKING ABOARD YOUR RV by Janet Groene. McGraw-Hill
   Company, P.O. Box 547, Blacklick, Ohio 43004 1-800-262-4729

COOKING ON THE GO by JoAnna M. Lund. Healthy Exchanges,
   P.O. Box 80, DeWitt, Iowa 52742 1-800-766-8961

EASY RV RECIPES by Ferne Holmes. Golden West Publishers,
   4113 N. Longview Avenue, Phoenix, Arizona 85014 1-800-658-5830

FAVORITE RECIPES FROM AMERICA'S CAMPGROUNDS by
   Ann Emerson, ed. Woodall Publications Corp., 2575 Vista Del Mar
   Drive, Ventura, California 93001 1-800-323-9076

GOOD STUFF COOKBOOK (on CD) by Cindy Michaels and Mike
   Hinkle. Cruising America, 1129 N. Minnesota, #361, Brownsville,
   Texas 78521 956-831-8494

THE HAPPY CAMPER'S GOURMET COOKBOOK by Joyce Ryan.
   Butterfly Books, 4210 Misty Glade, San Antonio, Texas 78247. (See
   the last page of this book for ordering information.)

THE RV COOKBOOK by Amy Boyer and Daniella Chace. Prima
   Publishing, 3000 Lava Ridge Court, Roseville, California 95661
   1-800-632-8676

A TASTE OF CIRCLE RV RANCH by Tweet Brumaghim. Circle RV
   Ranch, 1835 East Main Street, El Cajon, California 92021 1-800-
   422-1835

RV/CAMPING WEBSITES

The internet offers a volume of useful information for RVers. Websites feature: manufacturers, equipment, campgrounds, national and state parks, and personal advice from experienced RVers. Websites often have links to clubs, magazines, and events. Here are some of the many sites to surf:

www.americanjourneys.com
www.allcampgrounds.com
www.camping.about.com
www.campingontheinternet.com
www.thecampingsource.com
www.campingtime.com
www.camping-usa.com
www.campingworld.com
www.campnetamerica.com
www.cruising-america.com
www.escapees.com
www.fabuloustravel.com/campers
www.freecampgrounds.com
www.fulltiming-america.com
www.funoutdoors.com
www.funroads.com
www.fs.fed.us (National Forest Service)
www.fws.gov (U.S. Fish and Wildlife Service)
www.gocampingamerica.com
www.gorp.com
www.go-rv.com
www.gorving.com
www.gottarv.com
www.koa.com
www.lovetheoutdoors.com
www.movinon.net
www.newrvers.com
www.nps.gov (National Park Service)
www.recreation.gov
www.rvadvice.com

www.rvamerica.com
www.rvbookstore.com
www.rvcamping.com
www.rvclub.com
www.rv.com
www.rvdoctor.com
www.rverscorner.com
www.rversearch.com
www.rversonline.org
www.rvforums.com
www.rvjokes.com
www.rvlink.com
www.rvhome.com
www.rvhometown.com
www.rvia.org
www.rvingwomen.com
www.rvnet.com
www.rvonthego.com
www.rv.org
www.rv-portal.com
www.rvtoday.com
www.rvtraveler.com
www.rvusa.com
www.rvvideomagazine.com
www.rvzone.com
www.smartrvclub.org
www.tldirectory.com
www.usparks.about.com
www.webeuhcampin.com
www.womensrvforum.com
www.woodalls.com
www.workamper.com
www.workersonwheels.com

BIBLIOGRAPHY

Fox, Lori, ed. BETTY CROCKER'S GOOD AND EASY COOKBOOK. New York: Macmillan. 1996.

Kozar, Jean E., ed. BETTY CROCKER'S NEW COOKBOOK. New York: Macmillan. 1996.

Rombauer, Irma S., Marion Rombauer Becker, and Ethan Becker. JOY OF COOKING. New York: Scribner. 1997.

Ryan, Joyce. THE HAPPY CAMPER'S GOURMET COOKBOOK. San Antonio: Butterfly Books. 1992.

INDEX

A

After-Dinner Mint
   Tart, 173
Alfredo Sauce, 117
Aloha Pie, 170
America's Best
   Brownies, 162
   Hamburgers, 95
Apple Pie,
   Butterscotch-
      Pecan, 172
Austrian Hazelnut
   Torte, 179

B

Bacon
   and Potato Salad, 134
   -Tomato Spaghetti, 48
   -Wrapped Chicken, 60
   -Wrapped Shrimp, 88
Baja Sauce, 85
Baked beans--see beans
Baked Cajun Po' Boys, 83
Baked Chicken
   with Colorado Sauce, 61
   and Sausage Jambalaya, 59
Baked Corn Tortilla
   Strips, 39
Baked Polenta, 142
Baking pan substitutions, 191
Banana
   Brownies, 166
   Corn Bread, 37
Bar cookies
   Brownies--see Brownies
   Candied Fruit Bars, 166
   Cheesecake brownies--see
      Cheesecake brownies
   Peanut Butter Brownies, 168

White Chocolate-
   Almond Blondies, 167
Barbecue sauces
   Caribbean, 69
   Florida-Style, 65
   Kentucky Whiskey, 51
   Texas-Style, 63
Basic recipes, 193
Basil
   -Garlic Mashed Potatoes, 145
   Oven-Fried Potatoes, 143
   Tartar Sauce, 83
Beans, baked
   Bourbon, 136
Bean(s), black
   -Corn Salad, 126
   Dip, 16
   Rice and, 148
   Salad, 126
   Salsa Dip, 15
Beans, great northern
   Southwestern-Style Bean Dip, 18
Beans, green
   Herbed Bean Salad, 124
   Italian Salad, 125
   Italian Sauce, 67
   Two-Bean Salad, 125
Beans, red kidney
   Chili-Bean Hot Dogs, 93
   Herbed Bean Salad, 124
   Mexican Bean-Potato
      Salad, 133
   Mexican-Style Tossed Salad, 124
   Rice and Red Beans, 149
   Two-Bean Salad, 125
Beans, refried
   Frijoles Picante, 136
   Mexican Refried Bean(s), 137
   Soup, 115
   Toast, 137

Bean salad
  Black Bean, 126
  Black Bean-Corn, 126
  Herbed Bean, 124
  Italian Green Bean 125,
  Two-Bean, 125
Beef-Flavored Rice, 151
Beef, ground
  Hamburger Parmesan, 95
  Hamburgers--see Hamburgers
  Mexican Meat Loaf, 97
  Picante Chili, 114
  Ranch House Beef and Beans, 96
  Southwestern-Style
    Cocktail Meatballs, 98
    Meatballs, 98
    Spaghetti and Meatballs, 98
  Tex-Mex Sloppy Joes, 96
Beef, roast
  Deli-Style, 49
  Oven-Barbecued, 50
  Slow Cooker Carne
    Guisada, 50
  Smoky Oven-Barbecued, 50
Beef, sirloin steak
  Caribbean Fajitas, 55
  Grecian Skillet, 53
  Italian Breaded Panfried, 54
  Italian Herbed, 52
  Kansas City Broil, 55
  Kentucky-Style Barbecued, 51
  London Broil, 54
  and Potato Salad, 57
  Stir-Fried Fajitas, 56
  Taco-Flavored Kabobs, 53
  Zesty, 52
Black beans--see Beans,
  black
Blackened Hamburgers, 94
Black-eyed peas
  New Year's Day Dip, 16
  Texas Caviar, 17
Black Forest Bread, 27

Black Olive Oven-Fried
  Potatoes, 143
Black Walnut Brownies, 162
Blueberry Cheesecake
  Coffee Cake, 28
Blueberry Upside-Down
  Cake, 177
Blue Cheese
  Butter, 138
  -Garlic Cheese Ball, 15
Bourbon Baked Beans, 136
Bread, quick
  Black Forest, 27
  Hummingbird, 25
  Peanut Butter, 24
  Praline, 26
  Toffee, 26
Bread, yeast
  Coiled Bread, 45
  English Muffin Bread
    Cinnamon-Raisin, 47
    Oat Bran, 47
    Oatmeal, 47
    Whole Wheat, 47
  Focaccia, 44
    Herb, 44
    Italian Herb, 44
    Onion, 44
    Pesto-Topped, 45
    Southwestern, 44
  Rosemary, 46
  Thyme, 46
Broccoli-Cauliflower Gratin, 137
Brownie Liqueur Pie, 169
Brownies
  American's Best, 162
  Banana, 166
  Black Walnut, 162
  Butterscotch Cheesecake, 165
  Cherry-Almond, 162
  Chippety, 162
  Chocolate Cheesecake, 164
  Chocolate Fruitcake, 162

Chocolate Fruitcake, 162
Chocolate-Peanut Butter, 162
Chunky, 163
Coconut, 163
Date-Nut, 163
Maple-Pecan, 163
Mexican, 163
Mocha, 163
Peanut Butter, 168
  -Chocolate Chip, 168
  and Jelly, 168
Peanut Butter
  Cheesecake, 165
Raspberry Marbled, 163
Rum-Raisin, 163
Snickerdoodle, 163
Toffee, 165
Toffee Cheesecake, 165
Butter
  Blue Cheese, 138
  Mexican, 138
  Mustard, 104
  Picante, 138
  Southwestern, 138
  Taco, 138
Buttered Pecan Cheesecake, 184
Buttered Pecans, 185
Butterscotch
  -Apple Coffee Cake, 28
  Cheesecake Brownies, 165
  -Pecan Apple Pie, 172

C

Caesar Chicken
  Salad, 71
  Wraps, 71
Cajun
  Baked Po' Boys, 83
  Fried Fish, 84
  Hamburgers, 94
  Hen, 76
  Oven-Fried Chicken, 58
  Oven-Fried Potatoes, 143

Pilaf, 148
Shrimp Wraps, 88
Cake
  Austrian Hazelnut
    Torte, 179
  Blueberry Upside-Down
    Cake, 177
  Candy Fruitcake, 176
  Cherry Upside-Down
    Cake, 177
  Chocolate-Speckled, 180
  Cranberry Upside-
    Down, 177
  Eggnog Loaf Cake, 178
  Flourless Chocolate, 176
  White Chocolate
    Shortcake, 175
California-Style Garlic
  Salad Dressing, 120
Campground information, 198
Candied Fruit Bars, 166
Candy
  Bar Sauce, 156
  Crispy, 157
  Crispy Peanut Butter, 157
  Fruitcake, 176
  Maple-Pecan Fudge, 158
Caramelized Onions, 139
Caraway Corn Bread, 36
Caribbean
  Barbecue Sauce, 69
  Chicken Kabobs, 69
  Fajitas, 55
  Pancakes, 34
Carne Guisada, 50
Carrot
  -Apple Salad, 127
  -Zucchini Slaw, 127
Casserole
  Mix-and-Match, 112
Cauliflower
  -Broccoli Gratin, 137

Cheese ball(s)
  Blue Cheese-Garlic, 15
  Gouda, 14
  Green Chile, 14
  Monterey Jack, 15
  Monterey Jack-Herb, 15
  Pepper-Jack, 15
  Pesto, 14
Cheesecake
  Blueberry Cheesecake
    Coffee Cake, 28
  Brownies
    Butterscotch, 165
    Chocolate, 164
    Peanut Butter, 165
    Toffee, 165
  Buttered Pecan, 184
  Irish Cream-Chocolate, 182
  Mint Chocolate Fudge, 181
  Nutella, 183
Cheesecake Tart,
  After-Dinner Mint, 173
Cheese Salad Dressing, 75
Cheesy Sauce, Easy, 117
Cherry-Almond Brownies, 162
Cherry Upside-Down Cake, 177
Chesapeake Bay Shrimp
  Cocktail, 21
Chicken
  Caribbean Kabobs, 69
  and Cheese Chimichangas, 73
  Chinese Salad, 74
  Fiesta Salad, 75
  -Green Onion Sauce, 68
  -Mushroom Sauce, 68
  Red Chili, 115
  Soft Tacos, 70
  Stroganoff, 68
  Tex-Mex Manicotti, 72
  Tortilla Soup, 113
  White Chili, 114

Chicken, boneless
  Bacon-Wrapped, 60
  Baked with Colorado
    Sauce, 61
  Caesar
    Salad, 71
    Wraps, 71
  Cajun Oven-Fried, 58
  Florida-Style Barbecued, 65
  French-Style, 66
  Greek Baked, 64
  Italian Breaded, 60
  Polenta Breaded, 67
  "Ritzy" Baked, 58
  Roman-Style, 66
  Tex-Mex Sandwiches, 64
Chicken, breasts
  Baked Chicken and
    Sausage Jambalaya, 59
  Chinese Baked, 62
  Southern Oven-
    Fried, 62
  Texas-Style Barbecued, 63
Chicken-Flavored Rice, 151
Chili
  Picante, 114
  Red Chicken, 115
  White, 114
Chili-Bean Hot Dogs, 93
Chili-Bean Sauce, 93
Chili-Flavored Oven-
  Fried Potatoes, 143
Chili-Onion Baked Fish, 80
Chinese
  Baked Chicken, 62
  Chicken Salad, 74
Chippety Brownies, 162
Chocolate
  Brownie Liqueur Pie, 169
  Brownies--see Brownies
  Cheesecake Brownies, 164

Cream Cheese Frosting, 180
Crumb Crust, 175
Flourless Chocolate Cake, 176
Fruitcake Brownies, 162
German Chocolate Chip
  Cookies, 160
Irish Cream Cheesecake, 182
Mint Chocolate Fudge
  Cheesecake, 181
Peanut Butter, 155
-Peanut Butter Brownies, 162
Speckled Cake, 180
Velvet, 155
Chocolate Chip
  Coffee Cake, 31
  Mexican Cookies, 161
  Peanut Butter Brownies, 168
Chowder
  Salmon, 116
Christmas Coffee Cake, 30
Chunky Brownies, 163
Cinnamon Chip Coffee Cake, 31
Cinnamon-Raisin English
  Muffin Bread, 47
Clam Carbonara, 87
Cocktail Sauce, 81
  Chesapeake Bay, 21
  Creamy, 81
  Mexican, 85
Coconut Brownies, 163
Coffee cakes
  Blueberry Cheesecake, 28
  Butterscotch-Apple, 28
  Chocolate Chip, 31
  Christmas, 30
  Cinnamon Chip, 31
  Pumpkin, 29
Coiled Bread, 45
Coleslaw
  Colorful, 128
  Pasta Salad, 132
  Salsa Slaw, 128
Colorado Sauce, 61

Colorful Coleslaw, 128
Cookie Pizzettes, 158
Cookies
  Bar cookies--see Bar
    cookies
  Brownies--see
    Brownies
  Cranberry-White Chocolate
    Chip, 160
  German Chocolate Chip, 160
  Mexican Chocolate
    Chip, 161
Corn
  Black Bean-Corn Salad, 126
  on-the-Cobb with
    Southwestern Butters, 138
  Southwestern Succotash, 152
  -Tomato Salad, 129
Corn Bread, 36
  Banana, 37
  Caraway, 36
  Herb, 36
  Honey, 37
  Lemon, 36
  New Mexican, 36
  Parmesan, 36
Corn Bread Waffles, 32
Cornflake-Crusted
  Fish, 81
Cornish Hen, Simon
  and Garfunkel, 76
Cottage Cheese-
  Dill Dip, 20
Crab Cakes,
  Quick-and-Easy, 87
Cranberry
  -Orange Relish, 119
  Salsa, 111
  Upside-Down Cake, 177
  Waldorf Salsa, 119
  -White Chocolate Chip
    Cookies, 160

206

Creamy
  Caesar Salad Dressing, 120
  Cocktail Sauce, 81
  Mashed Potatoes, 145
  Pesto Sauce, 141
  Stuffed Potatoes, 144
Creole Sauce, 89
Crescent rolls
  Chicken and Cheese
    Chimichangas, 73
  French-Style Pizza, 41
Crispy Candy, 157
  Peanut Butter, 157
Croutons
  Crispy, 122
  Extra-Crispy, 122
Crusts--see Pie crust
Cuban Sandwiches, 104
Cuban-Style Roast Pork, 104

D

Date-Nut Brownies, 163
Deli-Style Roast Beef, 49
Dessert Nachos, 156
Dessert sauces
  Candy Bar Sauce, 156
  Chocolate Velvet, 155
Dip
  Black Bean, 16
  Cottage Cheese-Dill, 20
  Hummus, 18
  Italian Parsley Sauce, 19
  New Year's Day
    Black-eyed Pea, 16
  Pico de Gallo, 20
  Salsa, 16
    and Black Bean, 15
    Veggie, 17
  Southwestern-Style Bean, 18
  Texas Caviar, 17
Dryness, 195

Duckling
  Peking Duck, 77

E

Easy Cheesy Sauce, 117
Eggnog Glaze, 178
Eggnog Loaf Cake, 178
Eggs
  Florida Sunshine
    Toast, 35
  Green Onion Omelet, 78
  Italian Poached, 79
  Mexican Poached, 79
  Picante Deviled, 20
  Tex-Mex Quiche, 78
Enchilada Sauce, 118
Equipment, 9-12
Equivalents, 186-191
  Metric, 192
Extra-Crispy Croutons, 122

F

Fajitas
  Caribbean, 55
  Pork, 101
  Stir-Fried, 56
  Turkey, 109
Fiesta Chicken
  Salad, 75
Fish
  Baked Cajun Po'Boys, 83
  Cajun Fried, 84
  Chili-Onion Baked, 80
  Cornflake-Crusted, 81
  Garlic, 84
  Greek-Style Baked, 80
  Herb-Crusted, 82
  Mexican Fried with
    Veracruz Sauce, 85
  Parmesan, 79

Salmon Chowder, 116
Substitution table, 190
Fish sauces--see
Seafood sauces
Florida
Style-Barbecued
Chicken, 65
Sunshine Toast, 35
Flourless Chocolate
Cake, 176
Flour Tortillas, 39
Focaccia--see bread, yeast
Frappuccino, 156
French Bread with
Southwestern Butter, 41
French Pizzettes, 40
French-Style
Chicken, 66
Pizza, 41
Frico, 21
Frijoles Picante, 136
Frosting, Chocolate
Cream Cheese, 180
Fruitcake, Candy, 176
Fudge, Maple-Pecan, 158

G

Garlic
Basil-Mashed Potatoes, 145
Fish, 84
Mashed Potatoes, 145
Shrimp, 92
German Beer Muffins, 24
German Chocolate Chip Cookies, 160
Gingerbread Pancakes, 33
Glaze
Eggnog, 178
Vanilla, 30
Gouda Cheese Ball, 14
Graham Cracker Crust, 175
Grecian Skillet Steak, 53
Greek
Baked Chicken, 64

Pizzettes, 40
Salad for Two, 123
-Style Baked Fish, 80
-Style Shrimp, 92
Tomato Sauce, 92
Vegetable Salad, 129
Green Chile Cheese Ball, 14
Green Olive Tartar Sauce, 83
Green Onion Omelet, 78
Grilled
Beef, ground--see Ham-
burgers
Beef, sirloin steak
Caribbean Fajitas, 55
Italian Herbed, 52
Kansas City Broil, 55
Kentucky-Style Barbecued, 51
London Broil, 54
Taco-Flavored Kabobs, 53
Zesty, 52
Chicken
Caribbean Kabobs, 69
Ham with
Honey Mustard, 101
Honey Salsa, 100

H

Ham
French-Style Pizza, 41
Grilled with
Honey Mustard, 101
Honey Salsa, 100
-Mushroom Manicotti, 99
-Tomato Sauce with
Spaghetti, 100
Hamburger Parmesan, 95
Hamburgers
America's Best, 95
Blackened, 94
Cajun, 94
Italian, 94
Hearts of Palm Tossed
Salad, 123

Hen, Cajun, 76
Hen, Cornish--see
  Cornish Hen
Herb(ed)
  Bean Salad, 124
  Corn Bread, 36
  -Crusted Fish, 82
  Focaccia, 44
  Spaghetti, 140
  Tartar Sauce, 82
High altitude, 196, 197
Honey
  Corn Bread, 37
  Mustard, 101
  Salsa, 100
Horseradish Sauce, 49
Hot Dogs, Chili-
  Bean, 93
Humidity, 196
Hummingbird Bread, 25
Hummus, 18

I

Irish Cream-Chocolate
  Cheesecake, 182
Italian
  Beer Muffins, 24
  Cocktail Meatballs, 106
  Green Bean Salad, 125
  Green Bean Sauce, 67
  Hamburgers, 94
  Herbed Steak, 52
  Herb Focaccia, 44
  Herb Meat Loaf, 108
  Meatballs, 106
  Nachos, 21
  Parsley Sauce, 19
  Pasta Salad, 131
  Pizzettes, 40
  Poached Eggs, 79
  Sausage-Pepper Pizza, 42

Squash Combo, 153
Wedding Soup, 113
Italian Breaded
  Chicken, 60
  Panfried Steak, 54
  Pork Tenderloin, 103
  Shrimp, 90
Italian-Style
  Rice Salad, 134
  Rice and Vegetables, 150
  Salsa, 135
  Scalloped Potatoes
    and Tomatoes, 146
  Tossed Salad, 123

K

Kabobs
  Caribbean Chicken, 69
  Taco-Flavored Beef, 53
Kansas City Broil, 55
Kentucky Pecan Pie, 171
Kentucky-Style Barbecued
  Steak, 51
Kielbasa, turkey
  Polenta with Sausage-
    Mushroom Sauce, 105
  Polenta with Sausage-
    Pepper Sauce, 105

L

Lemon
  Corn Bread, 36
  Cream Pie, 169
  -Maple Syrup, 33
Lime Cream Pie, 169
London Broil, 54
Low Country Shrimp Boil, 91
Low-Fat
  Ranch Salad Dressing, 121
  Taco Salad Dressing, 121

M

Macaroni-Olive Salad, 130
Mandarin Snow Peas, 152
Manicotti
  Ham-Mushroom, 99
  Tex-Mex Chicken, 72
Maple-Butter Syrup, 32
Maple-Pecan
  Brownies, 163
  Fudge, 158
Meatballs
  Italian, 106
  Italian Cocktail, 106
  Italian Sausage-Pepper Pizza, 42
  Italian Wedding Soup, 113
  Mexican Sausage-Pepper
    Pizza, 43
  and Red Pepper-Black Olive
    Sauce, 106
  Southwestern-Style, 98
  Southwestern-Style Cocktail, 98,
  Southwestern-Style Spaghetti
    and, 98
  and Tetrazini Sauce, 107
Meat loaf
  Italian Herb, 108
  Mexican, 97
Metric equivalents, 192
Mexican
  Bean-Potato Salad, 133
  Brownies, 163
  Butter, 138
  Chocolate Chip
    Cookies, 161
  Cocktail Sauce, 85
  Fried Fish with Veracruz
    Sauce, 85
  Mashed Potatoes, 145
  Meat Loaf, 97
  Pasta Salad, 130
  Poached Eggs, 79
  Refried Beans, 137

Refried Bean Soup, 115
Refried Bean Toast, 137
Sausage-Pepper Pizza, 43
-Style Tossed Salad, 124
Sundae, 157
Microwave S'mores, 159
Mincemeat
  Scones, 23
Mint Chocolate Fudge
  Cheesecake, 181
Mix-and-Match Casserole, 112
Mocha Brownies, 163
Monterey Jack
  Cheese Ball, 15
  -Herb Cheese Ball, 15
  Pepper-Jack Cheese Ball, 15
Muffins
  German Beer, 24
  Italian Beer, 24
  Pineapple-Coconut, 23
Mushrooms
  and Onions, 139
  Portobello Sauté, 138
  Risotto, 149
Mustard Butter, 104

N

Nachos
  Dessert, 156
  Italian, 21
  Mexican Sundae, 157
New Mexican Corn Bread, 36
New Year's Day Black-eyed
  Pea Dip, 16
Nutella Cheesecake, 183

O

Oat Bran English Muffin
  Bread, 47
Oatmeal English Muffin
  Bread, 47

Oat-Nut Pancakes, 32
Old-Fashioned
  Macaroni Salad, 132
  Potato Salad, 133
Omelet, Green Onion, 78
One-Crust Pie, 174
Onion(s)
  Caramelized, 139
  Focaccia, 44
  -Fried Rice, 151
  Mushrooms and Onions, 139
  Pan Bread, 38
  Texas-Style Onion Soup, 116
Onion-Flavored Oven-
  Fried Potatoes, 143
Orange Syrup, 35
Oriental
  Dressing, 74
  Sauce, 110
Oven
  -Baked S'mores, 159
  -Barbecued Roast Beef, 50
Oven-Fried
  Potatoes, 143
  Potato and Sweet Potato, 146
  Southern Chicken, 62

P

Pancakes
  Caribbean, 34
  Gingerbread, 33
  Oat-Nut, 32
  Pumpkin, 34
Paprika Breaded Turkey
  Cutlets, 108
Parmesan
  Corn Bread, 36
  Fish, 79
  -Garlic Breadsticks, 38
  Hamburger, 95
  Salad Dressing, 121

Spaghetti with Black
  Olives, 141
  -Topped Potatoes, 144
Pasta salad
  Coleslaw, 132
  Italian, 131
  Macaroni-Olive, 130
  Mexican, 130
  Old-Fashioned Macaroni, 132
Pasta sauces
  Alfredo, 117
  Chicken-Green Onion, 68
  Chicken Stroganoff, 68
  Creamy Pesto, 141
  Greek Tomato, 92
  Ham-Tomato, 100
  Italian Green Bean, 67
  Pesto, 141
  Red Pepper-Black Olive, 106
  Sausage-Mushroom, 105
  Sausage-Pepper, 105
  Southwestern-Style Tomato, 98
  Spaghetti, 118
  Tetrazini, 107
  Tomato-Artichoke, 140
  Tuna-Tomato, 86
Peanut Butter
  Bread, 24
  Brownies, 168
    -Chocolate Chip, 168
    and Jelly, 168
  Cheesecake Brownies, 165
  Chocolate Peanut Butter, 155
  Chocolate-Peanut Butter
    Brownies, 162
  Crispy Peanut Butter
    Candy, 157
  Scones, 22
Pecan(s)
  Buttered, 185
  Buttered Pecan
    Cheesecake, 184

Maple-Pecan Fudge, 158
Pies
  Butterscotch-Pecan
    Apple, 172
  Kentucky, 171
  Texas, 171
  Walnut-, 171
Praline Bread, 26
Toasted, 26
Peking Duck, 77
Pepper-Fried Rice, 151
Pepper-Jack Cheese Ball, 15
Pesto, 141
  Cheese Ball, 14
  Creamy Pesto Sauce, 141
  Rice, 150
  Salad Dressing, 121
  -Topped Focaccia, 45
Picante
  Butter, 138
  Chili, 114
  Deviled Eggs, 20
  Sauce, 90
Pico de Gallo, 20
Pie
  After-Dinner Mint
    Tart, 173
  Aloha, 170
  Brownie Liqueur, 169
  Butterscotch-Pecan Apple, 172
  Kentucky Pecan, 171
  Lemon Cream, 169
  Lime Cream, 169
  Texas Pecan, 171
  Walnut-Pecan, 171
Pie crust
  Chocolate Crumb, 175
  Graham Cracker, 175
  One-Crust, 174
  Two-Crust, 174
Pineapple-Coconut
  Muffins, 23

Pizza
  Crust, 42
  French-Style, 41
  Italian Sausage-Pepper, 42
  Mexican Sausage-Pepper, 43
  Vegetarian Mexican, 43
  Wheat Crust, 42
Pizzettes
  Cookie, 158
  French, 40
  Greek, 40
  Italian, 40
Polenta, 142
  Baked, 142
  Breaded Chicken, 67
  with Sausage-Mushroom
    Sauce, 105
  with Sausage-Pepper
    Sauce, 105
Pommes Anna, 142
Pork tenderloin
  Cuban Sandwiches, 104
  Cuban-Style Roast, 104
  Fajitas, 101
  Italian Breaded, 103
  Piccata, 102
  Slow Cooker Pork
    Chalupas, 102
Portobello Mushroom
  Sauté, 138
Potatoes
  Basil-Garlic Mashed, 145
  Creamy Mashed, 145
  Creamy Stuffed, 144
  Garlic Mashed, 145
  Italian-Style Scalloped
    and Tomatoes, 146
  Mexican Mashed, 145
  Oven-Fried, 143
  Oven Fried and Sweet
    Potato, 146
  Parmesan-Topped, 144

Pommes Anna, 142
Tuna-Salsa Potato Topper, 86
Potato salad
  Bacon and, 134
  Mexican Bean-, 133
  Old-Fashioned, 133
  Steak and, 57
Praline Bread, 26
Pumpkin
  Coffee Cake, 29
  Pancakes, 34

Q

Quiche, Tex-Mex, 78
Quick-and-Easy Crab
  Cakes, 87

R

Ranch House Beef and Beans, 96
Ranch Salad Dressing,
  Low-Fat, 121
Raspberry Marbled Brownies, 163
Red Chicken Chili, 115
Red Pepper-Black Olive
  Sauce, 106
Refried beans--see Beans,
  refried
Relish
  Cranberry Orange, 119
Rice
  Beef-Flavored Rice, 151
  and Black Beans, 148
  Cajun Pilaf, 148
  Chicken-Flavored, 151
  Italian-Style Salad, 134
  Italian-Style and Vegetables, 150
  Mushroom Risotto, 149
  Onion-Fried, 151
  Pepper-Fried, 151
  Pesto, 150

and Red Beans, 149
Santa Fe, 147
and Vermicelli, 147
Rice salad
  Italian-Style, 134
"Ritzy" Baked Chicken, 58
Roman-Style Chicken, 66
Rosemary
  Bread, 46
  Oven-Fried Potatoes, 143
Rum-Maple Syrup, 34
Rum-Raisin Brownies, 163
RV
  /Camping websites, 200
  Cookbooks, 199
  ovens, 12, 13
  refrigerators, 12, 13

S

Safety tips, 13
Salad
  bean--see Bean,
    salad
  carrot--see Carrot
  coleslaw--see Coleslaw
  corn--see Corn
  dressing
    California-Style Garlic, 120
    Cheese, 75
    Creamy Caesar, 120
    Oriental, 74
    Low-Fat Ranch, 121
    Low-Fat Taco, 121
    Parmesan, 121
    Pesto, 121
    Tarragon, 57
  main dish
    Caesar Chicken, 71
    Chinese Chicken, 74
    Fiesta Chicken, 75
    Steak and Potato, 57

mixed vegetable
  Greek, 129
pasta--see Pasta,
  salad
potato-see Potato,
  salad
rice
  Italian-Style, 134
tomato
  Corn-Tomato, 129
  -Green Pepper, 135
  Italian-Style Salsa, 135
tossed,
  Greek Salad for Two, 123
  Hearts of Palm, 123
  Italian-Style, 123
  Mexican-Style, 124
  with Shredded Cheese, 122
Salmon Chowder, 116
Salsa, 16
  and Black Bean Dip, 15
  Cranberry, 111
  Cranberry Waldorf, 119
  Honey, 100
  Italian-Style, 135
  Ketchup, 97
  Slaw, 128
  Tuna-Salsa Potato
    Topper, 86
  Veggie, 17
Sandwiches
  Baked Cajun Po' Boys, 83
  Cuban, 104
  Pork Piccata, 102
  Tex-Mex Chicken, 64
Santa Fe
  Rice, 147
  Roast Turkey, 111
Sauces
  Barbecue--see Barbecue
    sauces
  Chili Bean, 93

Colorado, 61
Creole, 89
Dessert--see Dessert sauces
Easy Cheesy, 117
Enchilada, 118
Horseradish, 49
Oriental, 110
Pasta--see Pasta,
  Sauces
Picante, 90
Salsas--see Salsas
Seafood--see Seafood
  sauces
White, 117
Sausage, kielbasa--see Kielbasa,
  turkey
Sausage-Mushroom Sauce, 105
Sausage-Pepper Sauce, 105
Sausage, turkey--see Turkey
  sausage
Scones
  Mincemeat, 23
  Peanut Butter, 22
  Wheat Germ, 22
Seafood sauces,
  Baja, 85
  Basil Tartar, 83
  Chesapeake Bay Cocktail, 21
  Creamy Cocktail, 81
  Cocktail, 81
  Green Olive Tartar, 83
  Herb Tartar, 82
  Mexican Cocktail, 85
  Tartar, 84
  Veracruz, 85
Shortcake, White
  Chocolate, 175
Shrimp
  Bacon-Wrapped, 88
  Cajun Wraps, 88
  Chesapeake Bay Cocktail, 21
  Garlic, 92

Greek-Style, 92
Italian Breaded, 90
Low Country Shrimp Boil, 91
Picante, 90
Tacos, 88
Simon and Garfunkel Cornish
  Hen, 76
Slow cooker
  Carne Guisada, 50
  Pork Chalupas, 102
Smoky Oven-Barbecued
  Roast Beef, 50
S'mores
  Microwave, 159
  Oven-Baked, 159
Snickerdoodle Brownies, 163
Snow peas
  Mandarin, 152
Soft Chicken Tacos, 70
Soup
  Italian Wedding, 113
  Mexican Refried Bean, 115
  Picante Chili, 114
  Red Chicken Chili, 115
  Salmon Chowder, 116
  Texas-Style Onion, 116
  Tortilla, 113
  White Chili, 114
Southern Oven-Fried Chicken, 62
Southwestern
  Butter, 138
  Corn-on-the-Cobb, 138
  Focaccia, 44
  Succotash, 152
Southwestern-Style
  Bean Dip, 18
  Cocktail Meatballs, 98
  Meatballs, 98
  Spaghetti and Meatballs, 98
  Tomato Sauce, 98
Spaghetti
  Bacon-Tomato, 48
  Ham-Tomato Sauce, 100

Herbed, 140
Parmesan with Black
  Olives, 141
Sauce, 118
Southwestern-Style and
  Meatballs, 98
Tomato-Artichoke Sauce, 140
and Tuna-Tomato Sauce, 86
Spread
  Hummus, 18
  Southwestern-Style Bean, 18
  Tomato-Garlic, 19
Squash
  Italian Squash Combo, 153
  Southwestern Succotash, 152
  -Tomato Medley, 153
Standard measurements, 193
Steak and Potato Salad, 57
Stir-Fried
  Fajitas, 56
  Italian Vegetables, 154
  Sweet Potatoes, 147
Substitutions, 186-191
  Baking pans, 191
  Fish Substitution Table, 190
Supplies, 6-9
Sweet potato
  Oven-Fried with
    Potato, 146
  Stir-Fried, 147
Syrup
  Lemon-Maple, 33
  Maple-Butter, 32
  Orange, 35
  Rum-Maple, 34

T

Taco(s)
  Butter, 138
  Low-Fat Salad Dressing, 121
  Shrimp, 88
  Soft Chicken, 70

Taco-Flavored Beef Kabobs, 53
Tarragon
  Dressing, 57
  Oven-Fried Potatoes, 143
Tartar Sauce, 84
  Basil, 83
  Green Olive, 83
  Herb, 82
Tetrazini Sauce, 107
Texas
  Caviar, 17
  Pecan Pie, 171
  -Style Barbecued Chicken, 63
  -Style Onion Soup, 116
Tex-Mex
  Chicken Manicotti, 72
  Chicken Sandwiches, 64
  Quiche, 78
  Sloppy Joes, 96
Thyme
  Bread, 46
  Oven-Fried Potatoes, 143
Timesavers, 194
Toasted Pecans, 26
Toffee
  Bread, 26
  Brownies, 165
  Cheesecake Brownies, 165
Tomato(es)
  -Artichoke Spaghetti Sauce, 140
  Bacon-Tomato Spaghetti, 48
  Corn-Tomato Salad, 129
  -Garlic Spread, 19
  -Green Pepper Salad, 135
  Italian-Style Salsa, 135
  Squash-Tomato Medley, 153
  Tuna-Tomato Sauce, 86
Tortilla(s)
  Baked Corn Tortilla Strips, 39
  Dessert Nachos, 156

Flour, 39
  Italian Nachos, 21
  Mexican Sundae, 157
  Soup, 113
  Wheat, 39
Tossed salad--see Salads,
  tossed
Tuna-Salsa Potato Topper, 86
Tuna-Tomato Sauce with
  Spaghetti, 86
Turkey, boneless
  Santa Fe Roast, 111
Turkey Cutlets,
  Paprika Breaded, 108
Turkey Fajitas, 109
Turkey, ground
  Italian Herb Meat Loaf, 108
Turkey, kielbasa--see Kielbasa,
  turkey
Turkey in Oriental Sauce, 110
Turkey sausage
  Italian Cocktail
    Meatballs, 106
  Italian Meatballs, 106
  Italian-Pepper Pizza, 42
  Italian Wedding Soup, 113
  Meatballs and Red Pepper-
    Black Olive Sauce, 106
  Meatballs and Tetrazini
    Sauce, 107
  Mexican-Pepper Pizza, 43
Turkey tenderloin
  Fajitas, 109
  in Oriental Sauce, 110
Two-Bean Salad, 125
Two-Crust Pie, 174

U

Upside-Down Cake
  Blueberry, 177

Cherry, 177
Cranberry, 177

V

Vanilla Glaze, 30
Vegetarian Mexican Pizza, 43
Veggie Salsa, 17
Veracruz Sauce, 85

W

Waffles,
  Corn Bread, 32
Walnut-Pecan Pie, 171
Websites, 200
Wheat Germ Scones, 22
Wheat Tortillas, 39
White Chili, 114
White chocolate
  -Almond Blondies, 167
  Cranberry-White Chocolate
    Chip Cookies, 160

Shortcake, 175
White Sauce, 117
Whole Wheat English
  Muffin Bread, 47
Wraps
  Caesar Chicken, 71
  Cajun Shrimp, 88

Y

Yeast breads--see
  breads, yeast

Z

Zesty Steak, 52
Zucchini
  Carrot-Zucchini Slaw, 127
  Italian Squash
    Combo, 153
  Southwestern
    Succotash, 152
  Squash Tomato
    Medley, 153

BUTTERFLY BOOKS

welcomes your comments and suggestions regarding
AMERICA'S BEST RV COOKBOOK.
Send comments to:

Butterfly Books
Attn: Editor
4210 Misty Glade
San Antonio, Texas 78247

ABOUT THE AUTHOR

Joyce Ryan combines her love of traveling and cooking by writing RV cookbooks. For her latest book, twenty years of camping trips throughout the United States, Alaska, and Canada provide her with the special skills and experience required to address the unique challenges of RV cooking. She is a critically acclaimed author with nine books to her credit and listed in Who's Who since 1998.

America's Best Cheesecakes

150 Delicious and Easy-to-Prepare Recipes

JOYCE RYAN

Attention Cheesecake Lovers!

At last there is a cookbook that makes baking a cheesecake a snap. AMERICA'S BEST CHEESECAKES by Joyce Ryan (Butterfly Books, retail $12.95) features 150 recipes with practical step-by-step instruction. A fabulous desert is ensured by following the author's "Ten Cheesecake Commandments," a summary of no-nonsense success tips. The book includes:

- **150 RECIPES**
- **EXTENSIVE COLLECTION OF FLAVORS**--Chocolate Fudge, Viennese Coffee, Peach Melba, Brandy Alexander, Toffee, Butterscotch Brownie, Peppermint Chocolate Chip, Orange Cappuccino, Cranberry Vanilla, Black Russian, Apple Pie, and many more...

- **CLASSIC CHEESECAKE**
  A truly "classic" recipe with 33 + variations
- **SIX-INCH CHEESECAKES**
  Great for gifts!
- **EASIEST-EVER GARNISHES**
  Transform a simple cheesecake into a culinary masterpiece.

$12.95

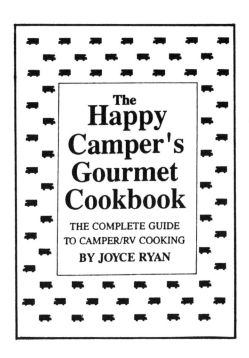

The
Happy
Camper's
Gourmet
Cookbook

THE COMPLETE GUIDE
TO CAMPER/RV COOKING
BY JOYCE RYAN

Discover Gourmet Camping!

"THE HAPPY CAMPER'S GOURMET COOKBOOK provides practical information and thoroughly tested recipes..."   CAMPING TODAY

"THE HAPPY CAMPER'S GOURMET COOKBOOK would be a welcome addition to any RVer's bookshelf."   WESTERN RV NEWS

"THE HAPPY CAMPER'S GOURMET COOKBOOK offers delicious easy-to-prepare food..."   RV TIMES MAGAZINE

Are you tired of boring casseroles and hot dogs? The gourmet quality recipes in THE HAPPY CAMPER'S GOURMET COOKBOOK (Butterfly Books, retail $11.95) are a snap to prepare and take into consideration the difficulties of limited space for both food preparation and for food storage. The book features 248 delicious recipes* and 39 menus.   200 pages

*NOTE: Only four of the recipes included in THE HAPPY CAMPER'S GOURMET COOKBOOK appear in AMERICA'S BEST RV COOKBOOK.   **$11.95**

**BUTTERFLY
B O O K S**

4210 Misty Glade
San Antonio, Texas 78247

ORDER FORM

Please send the following books:

Quantity	Title	Total
_____	America's Best RV Cookbook @$16.95	$_____
_____	The Happy Camper's Gourmet Cookbook @$11.95	$_____
_____	America's Best Cheesecakes @$12.95	$_____

Postage and handling   +$ 3.00

Texas residents add 7 3/4% sales tax
  ($1.31 for America's Best RV Cookbook
  $.93 for The Happy Camper's Gourmet Cookbook
  $1.00 for America's Best Cheesecakes)   + $_____

                                                                    Total $_____

Make check payable to BUTTERFLY BOOKS.
Mail book(s) to:

Name_____

Address_____

City/State/Zip Code_____

THANK YOU FOR YOUR ORDER!